Understanding Eng

Understanding English Grammar

A Course Book for Chinese Learners of English

Tony T. N. Hung

Hong Kong University Press
14/F Hing Wai Centre
7 Tin Wan Praya Road
Aberdeen
Hong Kong

© Hong Kong University Press 2005
First Published 2005
Reprinted 2008

ISBN-10: 962-209-726-X
ISBN-13: 978-962-209-726-1

All rights reserved. No portion of this publication may be reproduced or transmitted in any form or by any means, electronic or mechanical, including photocopy, recording, or any information storage or retrieval system, without permission in writing from the publisher.

Secure On-line Ordering
http://www.hkupress.org

British Library Cataloguing-in-Publication Data
A catalogue record for this book is available
from the British Library.

Printed and bound by Lammar Offset Printing Ltd., Hong Kong, China

Contents

Preface		vii
Introduction		1
1	The Subject	7
2	Nouns and Noun Phrases	21
3	Tense and Finiteness	41
4	Auxiliary Verbs and Aspect	57
5	Transitivity and Passive Voice	73
6	Verb Complementation	91
7	Simple Sentences	105
8	Finite Subordinate Clauses	117
9	Non-finite Subordinate Clauses	131
10	Relative Clauses	143
Notes and Answers Key		159
Appendices		221
	Writing tasks	221
	Proof-reading exercises	222
	Diagnostic test	223
Bibliography		233

Preface

Understanding English Grammar is a popular title and there are already a number of books in the market by that name. So what makes this book any different from the others?

Part of the difference is reflected by its subtitle: *A Course Book for Chinese Learners of English.* Virtually all other books on English grammar that I know of were written for readers with no particular language background in mind. They may (of course) be intended for learners of a particular level (intermediate, advanced, etc.), but I have rarely if ever come across a book which assumes readers with a particular first-language background, and which actually *exploits* that knowledge in explaining English grammar to them.

Regardless of the vicissitudes of Contrastive Analysis in the past 50 years, one basic tenet of the psychology of learning has remained unshaken, i.e. that previous learning influences subsequent learning, and in the case of language acquisition this is strikingly evident, not only in phonology but in syntax and semantics. To say that learners' errors and difficulties in the second language are not *fully* predictable or accountable with reference to their first language is not the same as saying that their first language does not exert a significant influence, both positively and negatively, on their acquisition of the second language.

I have written this book with the needs of Chinese-speaking learners of English in mind (having been one myself, and having taught them most of my life), in the belief that this has advantages with regard to clarifying and making easier certain key concepts and patterns in English grammar. But I want to emphasize that this is *not* a book on the Contrastive Analysis of English and Chinese. There are enough books of that kind and there is no need for me to add to their number. Rather than comparing English and Chinese grammar exhaustively, I have only drawn attention to those differences which matter most. But in spite of its focus on Chinese-speaking learners, this is first and foremost a book which attempts to present English grammar in a way which *makes sense*. It aims at helping learners of English to improve their understanding of English grammar through discovering its patterns and regularities for themselves.

The book originally arose from the observation that grammar is the weakest link in the overall language proficiency of many (if not most) of our learners of English, even after many years of communicatively oriented language learning. While there are many factors accounting for this state of affairs, and many possible solutions, my belief is that learners can benefit from a certain amount of explicit 'focus on form', as long as this is intended to supplement rather than supplant communicative language teaching.

Unlike some applied linguists and teachers, however, I do not see a need always to integrate grammatical instruction in the context of some communicative activity, as long as it does not become the main focus of language teaching but a supporting activity. In learning any other skills, such as playing the piano or tennis, teachers have no qualms about getting their pupils to practise particular scales or strokes (or any other forms), and the ultimate goal is never in doubt — i.e. to play the piano or tennis, not scales or strokes. Why should language teaching be any different, and why should teachers feel any qualms about focusing on form — or *forms*, when particular forms have proved to be problematic?

The underlying assumptions of the book are as follows:

(a) While the general orientation of language teaching should always remain 'communicative' (since language *is* communication), there is a legitimate place for 'focus on form' (which includes focus on grammar) in teaching and learning a language;

(b) Grammatical knowledge is best acquired if the learners work out systematic grammatical features for themselves and construct their own 'grammars' of the language on the basis of carefully selected, 'consciousness-raising' language data, and if this is followed up with practice on the forms in question;

(c) The learners' knowledge of their first language (in this case we have chosen to focus on Chinese) exerts a significant influence on their acquisition and conceptualization of the grammar of the second language (in this case English), and this prior knowledge should be duly taken into account in the teaching of the second language.

The book approaches English grammar neither prescriptively nor descriptively but inductively; and not by telling but by helping to discover. While there are many books available today which purport to help learners acquire a better understanding of English grammar, most of them adopt a straightforwardly explanatory or even prescriptive approach, and relatively few systematically require the learners to *think* about grammar and to come up with their own hypotheses about how it works on the basis of the given data. Even fewer directly address the needs of learners from a particular linguistic background and take full account of their first language in helping them understand how the second language works.

The book is designed for intermediate to advanced learners of English studying on their own, or with a teacher. Each chapter (or unit) is accompanied by a separate 'Notes for Students' section, which students can consult after working through all the data and exercises in each chapter, to check their own answers and to read further explanations on the grammatical points in question. Writing tasks, proof-reading exercises, and a diagnostic test to measure the students' progress, are also provided in the Appendices section at the end of the book, with an answer key. The book therefore appeals to the growing number of students learning English via self-access, as well as promotes independent learning among those who are enrolled in educational institutions.

In a book of this nature, it is always difficult to decide how much to include — English grammar being such a vast subject that it would be possible to write a 1700-page tome like Quirk et al.'s *Comprehensive Grammar of the English Language* and still feel that more is needed. This book is highly selective: it is not an 'A to Z' of English grammar, but focuses on those aspects of English grammar which have proved to be most problematic for learners of English as a second language, especially those from a Chinese-speaking background. I have based the selection of topics on my previous research on the 'interlanguage' grammars of first-year undergraduates at my university (the Hong Kong Baptist University; cf. Hung 2000), which has earlier formed the basis for a remedial grammar course which I designed for them. This course was a precursor of the present book, and I have benefited from the experience of teaching it for four years, and from the valuable feedback from my colleagues in the Language Centre. I wish particularly to thank Mr Leo Yu, Dr Carol Lam and Dr Mok Sui Sang for their helpful input and suggestions (in particular, Dr Lam provided the proof-reading exercises in the Appendices), and Ms Zhang Yanyan for her tireless editorial assistance. All the shortcomings of the book are, needless to say, entirely my own.

Introduction

What Is Grammar?

This book is about English grammar. We hope that, at the end of it, you will get a better understanding of how English grammar works, and that your own ability to use it will also be improved. But first, what do we mean by '**grammar**'?

We all know what words are. Here are a number of words from English:

met
she
yesterday
her friend

On their own, one at a time, words tell us very little. But here is the most powerful feature of all human languages — we can *combine* words to make **sentences**, which can tell us a lot more. For example, we can combine the above words to make strings of words like the following:

1. She met her friend yesterday.
2. Yesterday she met her friend.
3. She yesterday met her friend.
4. She met yesterday her friend, etc.

They all seem to mean something more than the words do on their own. Now, the important question is this: are the results always acceptable or **grammatical**?

QUESTION 1

Which of the above combinations (1–4) are acceptable or grammatical in English?

Answer:

[NB: When you see a double line like this, do not proceed further until you've answered the question.]

Most of you will have found only two of the four sentences above to be acceptable in English:

1. √ She met her friend yesterday
2. √ Yesterday she met her friend
3. * She yesterday met her friend
4. * She met yesterday her friend

[NB: From now on we'll use an asterisk * to indicate that a sentence is **unacceptable** or **ungrammatical**.]

 QUESTION 2

Can you say what is wrong with sentences 3–4 above?

Answer:

At this point some of you may be thinking to yourselves: Isn't the **meaning** of sentences 3–4 just as clear as in 1–2? May be so. But here is the important point: in English (as in any other language), it is *not* enough just to put words together to make meaning. To put it simply:

- **There are only certain ways in which words can be put together to form acceptable or 'grammatical' sentences.**

Other ways of putting words together (as in 3–4) are 'ungrammatical'. That is the first thing that we need to know about grammar.

Let's check this out further and compare how words are put together in another language, Chinese. We'll stick to the same combinations of words given in sentences 1–4. Try replacing each English word with an equivalent Chinese word, look at the results and mark each sentence below with a √ or * to show whether it is grammatical or ungrammatical *in Chinese*:

1. ___ She met her friend yesterday (Chinese: 她碰到了她朋友昨天)
2. ___ Yesterday she met her friend (Chinese: 昨天她碰到了她朋友)
3. ___ She yesterday met her friend (Chinese: 她昨天碰到了她朋友)
4. ___ She met yesterday her friend (Chinese: 她碰到了昨天她朋友)

What you have discovered about the above sentences will have led you to a second, equally important conclusion:

- **Different languages have *different* ways of putting words together.**

Our next step is to try and see if we can describe these differences. Our purpose is not to write detailed 'grammars' of English and Chinese, but to become more sharply aware that there are systematic differences between them, and to avoid making the mistake that what works in Chinese will work in English.

 QUESTION 3

Compare the Chinese and English sentences in 1–4 in terms of which combinations are grammatical or ungrammatical. What differences do you find?

English:

Chinese:

QUESTION 4

Now take each of the following sets of words, and try to combine them into sentences in both English and Chinese. Write out both the grammatical and ungrammatical combinations in each language:

1. *our teacher, left, the classroom, suddenly*
2. *I, bought, a house, last year*
3. *He, opened, the window, with a screwdriver*

	English	Chinese
Grammatical:	1. _____	_____
	2. _____	_____
	3. _____	_____
Ungrammatical:	1. _____	_____
	2. _____	_____
	3. _____	_____

Compare the grammatical and ungrammatical combinations in English and Chinese in the above examples. Try to think about them not as isolated examples, but as a group of data illustrating a particular *pattern* (or patterns*)* in the two languages. [NB: A 'pattern' is a *regular* 'behaviour' or way of doing things: e.g. in Hong Kong, you observe that all cars drive on the left side of the road, and that in mainland China, they drive on the right side. These are patterns.]

Try to describe these patterns in as clear and simple a way as you can. Don't worry if you don't have the technical vocabulary. All you need are basic, familiar terms like 'subject', 'verb', and 'object'. To start off, you can say something like this:

- In both English and Chinese, the subject regularly comes before the verb, and the verb regularly comes before the object.

(For instance, the subject 'I' comes before the verb 'bought', which comes before the object 'a house', in both English and Chinese.) Did you notice that particular pattern?

 QUESTION 5

Now go on to describe any other similarities or differences that you can find between English and Chinese grammar in the above examples.

Similarities:

Differences:

Summary

In this brief Introduction, you have seen that grammar is about the way the words of a language are put together to make sentences.

This is not as simple as it may seem — we can't simply put words together in a way that (we think) makes sense. The words have to be put together according to the 'rules' of grammar — and these 'rules' differ from language to language. What works in Chinese may not work in English!

In the rest of this book, we will try to discover what some of these rules are in English. 'Rules' in grammar are not rules made up by somebody to be obeyed by everybody else. These are just 'descriptions' or 'generalizations' of how the language works, how words are put together to form sentences in the language. They are patterns which you can discover for yourself (with a little help), and this book will help you to do that.

1

The Subject

Grammatical Properties

Let's consider these two sentences:

1. Singapore is the smallest republic in the world.
2. The smallest republic in the world is Singapore.

 QUESTION 1

The two sentences (1–2) are made up of exactly the same words, and they seem to be saying the same thing. But what is the **subject** of each of these sentences?

Sentence 1:

Sentence 2:

To put it simply, the subject is what the rest of the sentence is about. So, sentence 1 is about 'Singapore', and sentence 2 is about 'the smallest republic in the world'. The subject is one of the most important parts of a sentence in English — more so than in Chinese. To see how important it is, let's find out what sort of *grammatical properties* it has — that is, how does it behave in relation to the other parts of the sentence?

 QUESTION 2

In the following sentences, the subjects are underlined for you. What regular pattern can you see in the *position* of the subject in the sentence?

3. <u>China</u> has the largest population in the world.
4. <u>The concert by the youth orchestra</u> is completely sold out.
5. <u>The handsome frog</u> turned into an ugly prince.

Answer:

So you have worked out a simple 'hypothesis' about the position of the subject. But now consider the following sentences, where the subjects are again underlined.

6. As everyone knows, <u>China</u> has the largest population in the world.
7. To my disappointment, <u>the concert by the youth orchestra</u> is completely sold out.
8. Suddenly <u>the handsome frog</u> turned into an ugly prince.

 QUESTION 3

Do sentences 6–8 cause you to change the answer you gave to Question 2 above? If so, how?

Answer:

So you've noticed that the subject has a 'typical' position, namely at the beginning of the sentence and immediately before the verb. It is true that this is not the only possible position, as sentences 6–8 show. But you will note that if something else comes before the subject, it is normally not an *essential* part of the sentence: for example, if you delete everything before the subject in sentences 6–8, you are still left with a complete and grammatical sentence — i.e. sentences 3–5.

Let's look at some other properties of the subject besides its position. Consider sentences 9–12 below, and answer Questions 4 and 5:

9. <u>The little girl</u> *has* a big appetite.
10. <u>The little girls</u> *have* a big appetite.
11. <u>A tall building</u> *attracts* lightning.
12. <u>Tall buildings</u> *attract* lightning.

 QUESTION 4

Sentences 9–12 show an important grammatical property of the subject in English. What is that property? (Pay particular attention to the form of the verb that follows the subject.)

Answer:

QUESTION 5

What other grammatical property do you notice about the subject in the sentences below? [NB: Words like *be*, *have* and *can* are 'auxiliary verbs'. We'll explore them later.]

13. English *has* become a world language.
14. *Has* English become a world language?
15. Property prices *are* rising.
16. *Are* property prices rising?
17. Peter *can* eat 10 hamburgers in 1 minute.
18. *Can* Peter eat 10 hamburgers in 1 minute?

Answer:

To summarize the grammatical properties that you have discovered thus far about the subject in English:

(1) The subject usually occurs at the beginning of a sentence and before the verb;
(2) The subject controls the form of the verb in the present tense (singular/plural);
(3) The subject changes positions with the auxiliary verb in a question.

Except for (1), these properties of the subject are very different from Chinese.

What Does the Subject Actually 'Do'?

The above exercises have shown that the subject has certain **grammatical** properties — e.g. its position and relation to the verb, and so on. You will have noticed that it behaves differently from the subject in Chinese, e.g., in Chinese, the subject does not 'control' the form of the verb as it does in English (as in sentences 9–12), nor does it change positions with the auxiliary verb when asking a question (as in 13–18). In learning English, it is important to know these differences.

A different question about the subject is this: what does it actually 'do' in a sentence? Why do we need a subject at all?

Look again at sentences 1–18. You could say that the rest of the sentence is 'about' the underlined words — that is, about the subject. Without it, we would not know what the speaker is talking about, e.g.:

11. ? attracts lightning.
13. ? has become a world language.

 QUESTION 6

Identify and underline all the subjects in the following text. Do you agree that, in most cases, the rest of the sentence is 'about' the subject?

> Dictionaries are full of words, and words are common property. This sentence itself is made up of words which can all be found in any English dictionary — and yet the sentence is not common property. This is because words are not used in isolation, but are put together by the writer, and the resulting phrases and sentences are products of his mind. An idea may be quite commonplace: for example, the first sentence in this paragraph contains a perfectly common idea, which most of you will have thought of at one time or another. Yet the way the idea is expressed is entirely my own, and it is possible that no-one else has written exactly the same sentence before.

 QUESTION 7

In the following passage, the subjects have been left out from most of the sentences. Fill in the blanks with appropriate subjects:

> What is science? _____ is usually used to mean one of three things, or a mixture of them. _____ do not think _____ need to be precise — _____ is not always a good idea to be too precise. _____ means, sometimes, a special method of finding things out. Sometimes _____ means the body of knowledge arising from the things found out. _____ may also mean the new things _____ can do when _____ have found something out, or the actual doing of new things.
>
> (from Richard Feynman, *The Meaning of It All*)

As we have seen earlier, the subject normally tells us what the rest of the sentence is about, i.e. it is the 'topic' of the sentence.

But what if we already *know* what the topic is? For instance, in the following examples, do we really need to fill in the blanks with subjects in order to know what each sentence is about?

19. ___ is very hot in here.
20. ___ are lots of reporters outside.
21. A: What did Tom do last night? B: ___ went to a movie with his friends.

You will agree that, even without a subject, we can easily guess what each of the above sentences is about. In fact, in Chinese, we would not normally have a subject at all in sentences like 19, 20 and 21B. But in English, sentences 19–21B would be grammatically incomplete without a subject.

Here then is one important difference between English and Chinese:

- In English, a sentence *must* have a subject, even when the topic of discussion is clearly understood by the speaker and hearer;
- In Chinese, a sentence need not have a subject if the topic is understood.

In fact, think about the subjects in sentences 19–20:

19. It is very hot in here.
20. There are lots of reporters outside.

What do 'it' and 'there' tell us? Nothing really. They are 'empty' subjects — they are there only because the grammar of English *requires* a subject to be there!

So, in English, every sentence must have a subject. Usually, the **subject** is also the **topic** of the sentence, as in the following sentence, which is about Singapore:

21. Singapore is the smallest republic in the world.

Occasionally, the topic is different from the subject, and we see both of them side by side. In the following example, the topic is 'the crocodile', but the subject is 'nobody' (which controls the verb 'knows'):

22. As for **the crocodile**, nobody knows exactly where it is hiding.

It would be rather unusual to have a separate topic and subject both referring to the *same* thing (though it may not be ungrammatical):

23. As for **the property market**, it continues to fall.

This is not a normal kind of sentence, so don't overuse it. It sounds odd to say something like this (as many students do):

24. **Hong Kong people**, they are very independent.

'Hong Kong people are very independent' would have been more natural.

QUESTION 8

What is odd about the following sentences? Rewrite them properly.

1. In Graph 1, it shows that the standard of living in Hong Kong is rising.

   Answer:

2. According to the findings, they reveal that red wine is good for your health.

   Answer:

3. For this school, it was built 50 years ago, but still looks new.

   Answer:

4. Some people in the audience, they booed and shouted at the speaker.

   Answer:

Subject Omission

Earlier on, we said that a sentence must have a subject. There are times, however, when the subject may be left out in the second of two sentences (or main clauses) which are joined together. Consider the second half of the following sentences. They all have missing subjects, but some are grammatical while others are not.

 QUESTION 9

Mark each of the following sentences as either grammatical or ungrammatical (*). From these examples, can you explain when a subject can be left out and when it cannot?

1. He tried lifting the weight but was too heavy.
2. He tried lifting the weight but was too exhausted.
3. He couldn't lift the weight as was too heavy.
4. He couldn't lift the weight as was too exhausted.
5. She greeted us and sat down.
6. She greeted us before sat down.
7. He checked his pocket and was full of coins.
8. He checked his pocket and took out the coins.

The subject can be left out in the second clause if:
_____
_____

The subject cannot be left out in the second clause if:
_____
_____

Subject-Verb Agreement

There is a systematic feature of English grammar which is very simple to learn, but troublesome to remember, because it seems so 'unnecessary' that we don't miss it at all if it's not there — in fact, many languages, including Chinese, have nothing like it. This feature is 'subject-verb agreement', which we first saw in Question 4 above. Let's look at it more closely.

 QUESTION 10

From the following examples, can you give a simple explanation of how subject-verb agreement works?

1. The boy plays football every weekend.
2. The boys play football every weekend.
3. My father works in a library.
4. My parents work in a library.
5. Tom likes classical music.
6. Tom and Jerry like classical music.
7. Each student has a locker.
8. All students have lockers.

Answer:
_____
_____
_____

Now, what if the verb is in the past tense rather than present tense?

 QUESTION 11

Compare the following data with those in Question 10. How would you revise your earlier answer to give a more accurate account of subject-verb agreement?

9. The boy played football yesterday.
10. The boys played football yesterday.
11. My father worked in a library.
12. My parents worked in a library.
13. Tom liked classical music.
14. Tom and Jerry liked classical music.
15. Each student had a locker.
16. All students had lockers.

Answer:

If you think you have the right answers to Questions 10 and 11, then you have grasped the essence of the subject-verb agreement problem. But it's not enough just to know about it. You have to fully acquire the patterns for subject-verb agreement by giving yourself more practice, with exercises like the following:

 QUESTION 12

Fill in the blanks with the appropriate forms of the verbs in brackets, paying special attention to subject-verb agreement. Keep the verbs in the present tense.

1. My friends _____ (visit) me very often.
2. My best friend _____ (live) in the next block.
3. One of my friends _____ (be) a disc jockey.
4. Most of our teachers _____ (prefer) to teach in Chinese.
5. He _____ (spend) most of his money on CDs.
6. He and his wife _____ (spend) most of their money on CDs.
7. Many of the soldiers _____ (have) deserted.
8. One of the soldiers _____ (be) staying behind.
9. Each of these books _____ (cost) more than $200.
10. Few of these books _____ (cost) less than $250.
11. Most of the money _____ (have) been lost.
12. Most of the furniture _____ (have) been stolen.
13. Most of the students _____ (have) signed up.

Most of the time, subject-verb agreement seems very simple and straightforward. However, there are complications (as with many other aspects of grammar). The most troublesome cases of subject-verb agreement involve subjects which are more complex — e.g. a complex **noun phrase** such as 'The fierce leader of the resistance fighters' *was* (or *were?*) arrested'. We'll take up noun phrases in the next unit. In the Notes to this unit, we'll deal with some special cases of subject-verb agreement, if you're interested in reading more about it.

Additional Exercises

EXERCISE 1

In the following texts, most of the subjects have been left out. Fill in each blank with an appropriate subject, so that the sentence as a whole makes sense:

Text 1

Four men were attacked by a group of masked men wielding knives at Shamshuipo early on Thursday.

Around 12.39 am, _____ and _____ were talking on the corner of Shek Kip Mei Street and Fuk Wa Street.

"Suddenly, _____ jumped out of a private car and started attacking the victims," a police spokeswoman said.

_____ added: "After chopping them repeatedly, _____ fled in the private car on Boundary Road towards Kowloon City."

_____ were taken to Caritas Hospital for treatment.

Police said _____ did not know the men and had no idea why _____ were attacked.

Text 2

_____ and _____ were found burned alive in bed together yesterday after her former lover allegedly set light to her Tuen Mun home.

_____ had allegedly got into the woman's 21st-floor flat in Castle Peak Road after climbing in through the kitchen window at about 9 am.

"_____ allegedly poured gasoline into one of the bedrooms through the door gap when _____ were asleep inside," _____ said.

"_____ set the inflammable liquid alight and then ran out of the unit through the main door."

EXERCISE 2

Fill in the blanks with suitable verbs that fit the context, in the present tense if possible. Pay special attention to subject-verb agreement:

Text 1

There _____ many articles and letters in the *South China Morning Post* about the proposed ban on smoking in restaurants.

As a teenager, not only must I _____ second-hand smoke when I _____ out eating, but I also have to put up with it when I play sports in public playgrounds, play video games in a games centre, and when I surf the Net at Internet cafes.

I understand that a smoking ban _____ already in place in certain public areas; however, I see little being done to punish those who _____ the regulations.

Unless the government _____ to take action, for example, increasing fines for people who _____ the law, there _____ little point in extending the ban if smokers _____ to ignore it.

Text 2

Two men _____ been caught using a video camera to record a preview of a film — the first arrest of its kind since an amended copyright law came into effect in April last year.

The two, aged 26 and 27, _____ arrested at the Broadway Theatre in Sai Yeung Choi Street, Mongkok, during a preview of the Hong Kong-made action movie *So Close* on Saturday. They _____ caught with a digital video camera and two cassettes.

The new film _____ Taiwanese actress Shu Qi and *Shaolin Soccer's* Karen Mok Man-wai and Vicky Zhao Wei. It _____ on an international conspiracy involving murders and computer viruses.

Text 3

Cinemas _____ attendance levels to double from today when ticket prices _____ cut to $25 for films screened on Tuesdays and Wednesdays.

Box-office takings _____ slumped to record lows this summer, diving more than 45 per cent from $386 million last year.

In July last year, the local smash hits *Shaolin Soccer* and *Love on a Diet* together grossed $90 million, but this year the biggest releases, *Men in Black II* and *Minority Report*, _____ taken only half that amount.

2

Nouns and Noun Phrases

Introduction: Nouns and Things

You all know what **nouns** are. Here are some common nouns in English:

water, air, earth, rice, sand, gold, paper, money, time, advice, courage

As you learned in school long ago, nouns are names of 'things' — some we can touch, and some we can't. We can talk about any of them:

1. *Water* is hard to find in a desert.
2. *Rice* grows well in a hot, humid climate.
3. *Courage* is an admirable quality.

Notice that all the nouns in italics in the above examples can be used on their own in a sentence (without an article, etc.) — just as in Chinese. (Think of their Chinese equivalents and you will see.)

There is another thing that you should notice about nouns like the above: they all refer to things that do not have any *natural* shape, size, or boundary. Water is water. There can be a drop, a cupful, a tankful, or even an ocean of water, but it's still the same substance, water. There's no sense in talking about 'one water', 'two waters' and so on. The same goes for 'air', 'rice', 'paper', etc.

What happens if you do need to refer to a particular unit or quantity of water or rice or paper? You'll need a **'measure word'** of some sort, for example:

4. *A drop of water* cannot do much, but *a million drops of water* can.
5. There's not even *a grain of rice* left in the bowl.
6. How many *pieces of paper* do you need?

22   Understanding English Grammar

Again, this is just like Chinese. (Think of the equivalents for 'a drop of water', 'a grain of rice' and 'a piece of paper' in Chinese: '一滴水', '一粒米', '一張紙'.) Notice that, however large a quantity we may be talking about, the noun itself (*water, rice, paper*, etc.) does not change its form.

 QUESTION 1

Find appropriate measure words for the other nouns mentioned above, and use each of them in a sentence:

Air	_____
Earth	_____
Sand	_____
Gold	_____
Money	_____
Time	_____
Advice	_____
Courage	_____

So far, it would seem that at least some nouns in English behave very much like nouns in Chinese — in being able to occur on their own ('Water is precious'), and in needing a measure word when quantity is involved ('many drops of water'). If all English nouns were like that, it might be easier in a way, as all nouns would then be unchanging in form, as in the case of *water:*

  7. I can see *water* everywhere.
  8. *Water* is essential for life.
  9. After exercising, I have to drink a lot of *water*.

But are all nouns in English actually like that?

 QUESTION 2

Consider the underlined nouns in the following sentences (which are basically similar to 7–9). What's wrong with them? How would you correct them?

10. I can see <u>soldier</u> everywhere.
11. <u>Tree</u> is essential for parks.
12. After school, I have to read a lot of <u>book</u>.

Answer:

'Count' and 'Mass' Nouns

You have just identified a major difficulty about using nouns in English, i.e. how to distinguish between nouns like *water, rice* and *paper* on the one hand, and nouns like *soldier, tree* and *book* on the other. There's nothing quite like this in Chinese, where all nouns are essentially like *water, rice* and *paper* in the way they are used.

But at least you realize that in English it is nouns like *soldier, tree* and *book* that behave differently from nouns in Chinese, and may pose more of a problem. Let's call these nouns by their modern name, **count nouns** (or 'countable nouns') — nouns like *table, chair, house, car, flower, man, woman, teacher, school, month, year,* etc. The other group (*water* etc.) are **mass nouns** (or 'uncountable nouns').

 QUESTION 3

Compare the ways in which the nouns *money* and *flower* are used below. Write down all the grammatical differences that you find. Which is a count noun and which a mass noun?

Money

1. Money grows on trees.
2. *Moneys grow on trees.
3. *A money grows on trees.
4. Much/a little money is good.

Flower

*Flower grows on trees.
Flowers grow on trees.
A flower grows on trees.
Many/a few flowers are good.

Answer:

The differences between the two types of nouns are:

Mass Noun	Count Noun

The grammatical differences between count and mass nouns are relatively easy to describe (as you have done above). There is, however, no simple way of explaining why a noun behaves like a count or mass noun (or both). A good dictionary (such as the *Longman* or *Oxford Advanced Learners*) will label each noun as [C] (countable) or [U] (uncountable), according to its meanings. But are there any basic concepts which can help us distinguish the two, even if only roughly?

Try asking yourself this question:

- Does the noun refer to something that is *naturally* bounded? If so, it is more likely to be a count noun.

Think of something like 'time'. Time is open-ended and without a natural or inherent boundary. The word *time* is, not surprisingly, a mass noun. '*Time* is precious', 'I don't have much *time*', etc. Now think of a *bounded* segment of time: e.g. a second, a minute, an hour, a day, a week, a month, a year, a century. However long or short, each of them has an inherent boundary, unlike 'time' itself. Not surprisingly, they are count nouns. 'Do you have *a minute*', 'Many *days* later, he returned', etc.

 QUESTION 4

Does the above idea help you to see why each of the nouns below is a **count** noun or a **mass** noun? Divide them into these two groups.

water, lake, pond, sand, dune, money, dollar, cent, literature, novel, poem, vegetation, flower, tree, furniture, chair, table

Mass Nouns:

Count Nouns:

Number and Agreement

The distinction between 'count' and 'mass' nouns is not made just for fun. Whether a noun is a count noun or mass noun has some important consequences for the grammar of English. The most obvious is **number** — i.e. singular and plural forms of nouns:

- Count nouns have a **singular** form (e.g. *book*) and a **plural** form (e.g. *books*)
- Mass nouns only have a singular form

If you know that a certain noun is a count noun, number is usually a straightforward matter of adding a suffix *–s* to the plural form:

A book, one book   vs. *ten books, many books, a lot of books*
I like to read a book   vs. *I like to read books*

Though there are a small number of irregular nouns in English which form the plural differently (like *man~men, child~children*), it is just a matter of memorizing a list of such nouns. What is more important — because it is a *systematic* aspect of English grammar — is the fact that the form of the **verb** has to 'agree' with the **subject** in terms of **number** (singular or plural), if it is in the present tense, for example:

1. *The student* **drives** to school in a sports car.
2. *The students* **drive** to school in sports cars.

We have already touched on subject-verb agreement in Unit 1. It is one of those 'meaningless' things in English grammar which we have no choice but to learn — just because it is there. Fortunately, the concept is a very simple one, and again fortunately, agreement applies only in the present tense but not in the past tense in English (except for one single verb, *be*).

However, there's one major complication. A problem arises when the subject is not a single word but a **phrase**, e.g. 'one of the boys'. What should the verb agree with, 'one' or 'boys'? Should we say 'One of the boys *is* brilliant' or 'One of the boys *are* brilliant'? What about 'The boy who beat all his classmates'? Should the verb agree with 'boy' or 'classmates', and should we say 'The boy who beat all his classmates *is/are* brilliant'?

The Noun Phrase

At this point, we'll need to step back and look at the larger picture of words and phrases in English.

Most students tend to think of sentences as being made up of individual **words**. This, of course, *appears* to be true some of the time. For example, the subject of the sentence 'Girls are naughtier than boys' is the word (the noun) 'girls'.

However, the more you think about it, the more you will notice that words group themselves into **phrases**, and that, however long these phrases may be, they basically behave like one *single word*! For example, look at the underlined phrases in the following sentences. No matter how long or short, don't all the phrases seem to be built around one single noun?

(a) <u>The boy</u> is a genius.
(b) <u>The young boy</u> is a genius.
(c) <u>The young boy from Hong Kong</u> is a genius.
(d) <u>The young boy from Hong Kong who won the chess tournament</u> is a genius.

QUESTION 5

What is each of the underlined phrases in sentences a–d above basically about? Which of these phrases can be replaced by the pronoun 'he'?

Answer:

You will probably agree that each of the underlined phrases in sentences a–d is about a certain 'boy' (and not about 'Hong Kong' or a 'chess tournament'). All the other words in the phrase tell us something more about this 'boy' — e.g. 'young' (the *boy* is young), 'who won the chess tournament' (the *boy* won the chess tournament), and so on.

So, in a very real sense, the noun 'boy' is the **head** of the whole phrase. And since the head is a noun, the whole phrase behaves like a noun too, which is why, no matter how long the phrase is, it can be replaced by a pronoun like 'he'. Let's therefore call the whole phrase a **noun phrase**. All the underlined groups of words in sentences a–d are noun phrases, and the whole noun phrase (not just the noun) is the **subject** of the sentence.

It is not necessary to go too deeply into the structure of the noun phrase here, but just to give a brief overview:

(a) a noun phrase (obviously) has a **noun** as its **head**.
(b) In addition, it may have a **determiner** (like 'the' in 'the boy') and one or more **adjectives** (e.g. 'young') before it.
(c) It may also have other words *following* it, such as a **prepositional phrase** (e.g. 'from Hong Kong') and a **relative clause** (e.g. 'who won the chess tournament').

We'll have more to say about the determiner later on in this unit, and about the relative clause in Unit 10. For now, here's a summary of what a complex noun phrase may contain:

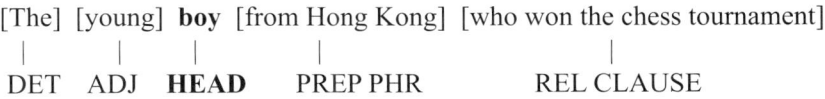

```
[The]  [young]  boy   [from Hong Kong]  [who won the chess tournament]
  |       |      |           |                        |
 DET    ADJ    HEAD      PREP PHR                REL CLAUSE
```

Subject-Verb Agreement Revisited

Let's return now to the old problem of subject-verb agreement. If the subject of a sentence is a complex noun phrase instead of a simple noun, *what* does the verb agree with?

 QUESTION 6

The subject of each of the following sentences is a noun phrase (enclosed in square brackets for easy identification). In each noun phrase there are two or more nouns (given in **bold** print). Underline the noun which seems to you to control agreement with the verb.

1. [The **leader** of the **rebels**] has surrendered.
2. [The newly-elected **spokesman** for the **workers**] seems very inexperienced.
3. [The former **lovers** of the **president**] have come forward one by one.
4. [The **players** who lost to the **newcomer**] were taken by surprise.
5. [The **disease** which struck fear in **millions** of **people**] was SARS.

If you have chosen the correct answers in the above exercise, then the nouns that you underlined are the heads of the noun phrases. Yes, the **head** of a noun phrase controls subject-verb agreement, and not any other noun in the noun phrase. This seems reasonable enough, since the head is what the whole noun phrase is all about.

If this seems simple enough to you, then why do students still make so many mistakes with it? To say that the verb must agree with the head of the noun phrase is easy, but it may not be that easy for the learner to decide *which* noun is the head!

In Chinese, the head of a noun phrase is very easy to identify. It always occurs at the *end* of the noun phrase. So instead of [the young **boy** who won the chess tournaments], we have something like:

[the won the chess tournaments young **boy**] is a genius.
〔那個贏了象棋比賽的男孩〕是位天才

In that case, subject-verb agreement would be very simple, as the verb would always agree with the noun *immediately before* it (e.g. 'boy')!

But English grammar, unfortunately, does not work like that. The noun head in English may not be at the end of the noun phrase and closest to the verb — as in '[the *boy* who won the chess tournaments] is a genius', where the verb 'is' is separated from the noun head 'boy' by several other words. So, to identify the noun head in an English noun phrase, you should always ask yourself, what is the whole phrase about? For example, is it about a certain 'boy', or about 'chess tournaments', or something else?

QUESTION 7

In the following examples, put brackets around the whole **noun phrase**, and underline the **noun head**; also, give the correct present-tense form of the verb (in brackets) such that it agrees with the noun head.

1. The schedule showing the jetfoil arrivals and departures _____ (be) out-of-date.
2. His book of old photographs _____ (be) missing.
3. The recent development of new public facilities _____ (have) led to an increase in tourism in the area.
4. The trees in the park _____ (need) trimming.
5. The floods which hit Hunan Province recently _____ (have) caused untold damage.
6. The search for the terrorists _____ (go) on.
7. The new neighbour who moved in yesterday with 11 dogs _____ (seem) a little weird.
8. The Olympic athlete with the greatest number of gold medals _____ (be) Mark Spitz.
9. A car with four doors _____ (cost) a little more than one with two.
10. The mathematician whose Nobel Prize surprised many people _____ (be) John Nash.

The Determiner

Now that we've introduced the concept of the noun phrase, let's look more closely at one of the most important parts of a noun phrase, which is the cause of a different kind of problem in the use of nouns and noun phrases by Chinese learners of English.

If you open an English dictionary, you will find entries like the following for nouns like *car* and *policeman*:

Car: *n.* motor vehicle with four wheels for carrying passengers
Policeman: *n.* male member of the police force

Notice that, in their bare form (i.e. 'car' or 'policeman'), these words refer to a *type* of object or person. 'Car' is a type of vehicle, and 'policeman' is a type of person. They do not refer to any actual, individual car or policeman in this world.

Therefore, when you use these nouns in their bare form in an actual sentence, there is something odd about it:

1. * I saw *car* in the garage yesterday.
2. * The robber shot *policeman* outside the bank.

When you see something, you see an actual object and not a type of object, and when you shoot somebody, you shoot an actual person, not a type of person!

 QUESTION 8

What sort of words would you put before the nouns in the following sentences to make them sound right? (Think of as many different words as you can.)

---

3. I saw _____ car in _____ garage yesterday.
4. _____ robber shot _____ policeman outside _____ bank.
5. _____ friend works in _____ restaurant.
6. _____ teacher gave _____ very boring lecture today.

 **QUESTION 9**

Why do you think the words that you used to fill in the blanks in Question 8 are needed? (There's no need to give a technical answer here — just use your own words.)

Answer:

Perhaps the basic idea is becoming clear to you now. A noun by itself (like 'car') only refers to a type of thing. To use it to refer to an individual thing in the real world, you will need to 'limit' it in some way, from a type to an individual case (out of the millions of possible cases). And what kind of word do we use for this purpose? The kind of words that you used to fill in the blanks in Question 8. Here are some possibilities for 'car' in sentence 3:

I saw	*a car* *the car* *this car* *that car* *her car* *your car* *etc.*	in the garage yesterday

Each of these words — *a, the, this, that, her, your,* etc. — 'limits' the noun *car* in some way, so that it refers to an individual car, and not just a type of object called 'car'.

Such words are known as **determiners**. Other words, like *each, every, some, one, two,* etc., which refer to quantity, also act as determiners.

Nouns and Noun Phrases 31

 QUESTION 10

Underline all the determiners in the following paragraph.

> Once upon a time, there was an old man in Northern China called Yu Gong ('Foolish Old Man'). In front of his house stood two tall mountains. To go to the nearest town, Yu Gong had to go around these mountains, which took a long time. So one day he called his family together, and announced that they would start digging and removing the mountains. He said, 'When my sons and I are dead and gone, their sons will carry on, and their sons and their sons …'

Earlier on in this unit, we made a distinction between count nouns and mass nouns. Count nouns have a singular and a plural form (e.g. *house* and *houses*), while mass nouns only have a singular form (e.g. *gold*). Now here is another grammatical difference between the two:

   A **singular count noun** *must* take a determiner

Thus, it would not be grammatical to say *'This is house'. The singular count noun *house* must take a determiner, such as 'This is *a/the/my/his* house'. On the other hand, a singular mass noun, and a plural count noun, need not take a determiner (although they can): 'This is gold', 'These are houses', etc. are grammatical.

 QUESTION 11

In the following passage, some determiners have been left out. Fill in the blanks with a suitable determiner *only where necessary*.

> After waiting for several years, ____ friend finally decided to buy ____ DVD-player. He waited for such ____ long time because of ____ coding system which makes ____ DVDs from ____ different parts of ____ world incompatible, which is ____ terrible nuisance. Later on, ____ DVD-players which can play all codes became available, and that solved ____ problem. He now rents and watches ____ movie every day.

The Article

By far, the most common determiners in English are the **articles**, namely *a (an)* and *the*. Many mistakes are made by students who choose the wrong article, and part of the reason may be that there are no real articles in Chinese. (There are Chinese words which are equivalent to 'one' and 'that', but nothing equivalent to 'a' and 'the'.)

You all know that *a* is known as the '**indefinite** article', and *the* as the '**definite** article'. It is not that simple to explain how they are used. Forget about the definitions you've learned for the moment, and try to analyse the following texts for yourself.

 QUESTION 12

Underline all the definite and indefinite articles in the text below, and explain the choice of each of these articles in this context.

> I've bought a new car. It is a Mazda sports car. It has a slim body and a powerful engine. The engine is turbo-charged, and the car can accelerate from 0 to 100 kph in 5 seconds.

(i) The indefinite article *a/an* is used when:

(ii) The definite article *the* is used when:

I'm sure you've found the above example relatively easy to explain. It seems quite straightforward when to use the definite or indefinite article — or does it?

 QUESTION 13

Underline all the definite and indefinite articles in the following text. Does the explanation you have given above explain the choice of articles here? If not, how can you explain these other uses of the articles?

> I've bought a new car. The engine is turbo-charged and super powerful. The bumpers are made of a special material which can stand the severest punishment. The seats are made of the best leather, and are electrically operated.

Answer:

You will have realized by now that it is not that easy and straightforward to explain when you can use the indefinite article *a* and the definite article *the*. To say that you use an indefinite article when you mention a noun for the first time in a text, and the definite article when you mention it again, is obviously not enough.

Rather than overwhelm you with a massive number of 'rules', you will learn more if you analyse and discuss with your classmates and teachers more examples of the correct and incorrect uses of the articles, and try to understand as much of this as you can. The questions below are designed to help you do this.

 ## QUESTION 14

Though it is true that you generally use the definite article *the* when you refer to a noun already mentioned before, it is of course not limited only to such cases. Consider the use of the definite article in the following examples. Why do you think *the* is used, even though the noun is mentioned for the first time?

1. Do you have the key?
2. Where's the switch?
3. Turn on the light.
4. Open the door.
5. He went to the library.
6. Call the police!
7. He complained to the manager.
8. She is at the airport.
9. What's the time?
10. What's the problem?

Answer:

 QUESTION 15

Compare the following pairs of sentences (a/b), where an indefinite article is used in the first and a definite article in the second. Can you explain why the definite article is needed in the (b) sentences but not in (a)?

(1a) This is an interesting book.
(1b) This is the most interesting book I have ever read.

(2a) I bought a book on astrology.
(2b) I bought the only book on astrology in the bookstore.

(3a) I had a girlfriend in school.
(3b) She was the first girlfriend I ever had.

(4a) He found a key in his pocket.
(4b) He found the key to the safe in his pocket.

Answer:

 **QUESTION 16**

In the following pairs of sentences (a/b), the same noun is used with or without a definite article. Is there a difference in meaning between the two sentences? If so, explain the difference.

(1a) He loves children.
(1b) He loves the children.

(2a) Where can I buy DVDs?
(2b) Where can I buy the DVDs?

(3a) He kept stray dogs as pets.
(3b) He kept the stray dogs as pets.

(4a) They imported rice from Thailand.
(4b) They imported the rice from Thailand.

(5a) He found money under his bed.
(5b) He found the money under his bed.

Answer:

36 Understanding English Grammar

 QUESTION 17

The following sentences were written by students. Identify and correct any errors that you find in their use of articles.

1. The majority of respondents agreed.
Correction: _____

2. Most of plants were giant plants.
_____

3. All of them agreed that ability to communicate was important.
_____

4. The vitamin can inhibit development of cancer.
_____

5. It contains large amount of carotene.
_____

6. It is used by human body.
_____

7. We should save the energy as much as possible.
_____

8. The layer of the mud became hard rock.
_____

Recapitulation

To recapitulate, in this unit, you saw that a **noun phrase**, however long, behaves just like a single **noun**. Thus, in the sentence:

<u>The powerful **typhoon** which swept past Hong Kong last week</u> did not cause too much damage.

the whole underlined phrase (the powerful **typhoon** which swept past Hong Kong last week) is a noun phrase, and it can be replaced by a pronoun 'it', just like any other noun. We'll summarize below what a noun phrase is made up of. First, and most obviously, it must have a **noun** — e.g. 'typhoon'. This is the '**head**' of the noun phrase: as we have seen in this unit, the noun head is what the whole noun phrase is all about, and it controls **agreement** with the verb.

Besides the head, a noun phrase may also have the following parts:

(a) BEFORE THE NOUN:
  (1) A **determiner** — e.g. '*the* **typhoon**'
  (2) One or more **adjectives** — e.g. 'the *powerful, swift* **typhoon**'

(b) AFTER THE NOUN:
  (3) A **prepositional phrase** — e.g. 'the powerful **typhoon** *from the south*'
  (4) A **relative clause** — e.g. 'the powerful **typhoon** *which swept past Hong Kong last week*'

We'll look more closely at relative clauses later on in this course. Right now, the important thing is to learn to look at the whole noun phrase as one single unit, and to know where to look for the **noun head**.

To round off this unit and consolidate what you have learnt, here are some more exercises to sharpen your recognition of the noun phrase and noun head, and practise your use of articles and determiners.

Additional Exercises

EXERCISE 1

In each of the sentences below, the subject is a **noun phrase**. Put square brackets around the whole noun phrase, underline the **noun head**, and fill in the blank with the correct form of the verb given in brackets.

Example: The film which won the greatest number of Academy Awards _____ (be) Lord of the Rings 3.

Answer: [The <u>film</u> which won the greatest number of Academy Awards] was *Lord of the Rings 3.*

1. The first anniversary of the Sept. 11 terrorist attacks _____ (be) commemorated all over the world.
2. The families of the victims _____ (be) invited to attend memorial services in New York, Washington and Pennsylvania.
3. The names of all those who died in the World Trade Centre _____ (be) read out by the former mayor of New York, Rudy Giuliani, and others.
4. Documentaries on the attacks and their aftermath _____ (be) shown on TV in Hong Kong.

5. The documentary which caught the attention of most viewers _____ (be) about a young fireman on his first job in New York.
6. The cameramen who shot this documentary _____ (be) two French brothers.
7. The film which they shot inside the World Trade Centre during the attack _____ (be) the only one of its kind.

> EXERCISE 2

In the following texts, some of the articles and other determiners have been left out. Fill in the blanks with suitable articles/determiners (*a, the, this, that, his, her, their* etc.), *only if one is needed*. Compare your answers with your classmates' and teachers', and discuss any problems or disagreements that you may have — especially if you are unable to understand why a certain determiner should or should not be used.

Text 1

_____ evidence is growing of _____ link between global warming and _____ floods and droughts that devastated parts of Asia, southern Africa and Europe _____ year, _____ head of _____ United Nations' body on climate change said yesterday.

Rajendra Pachauri, chairman of the Inter-governmental Panel on Climate Change, told summit delegates there was undeniable proof that _____ Earth was warming.

"I think the evidence is becoming stronger that _____ lot of these extreme [weather] events are part of _____ overall process of climate change ... there is _____ fair amount of statistical evidence and there is certainly anecdotal evidence ... and I think _____ indications are that there is _____ link there."

Text 2

_____ love-struck Chinese couple handcuffed themselves to each other during _____ tour outing and ended up being stopped by _____ policemen after _____ tourist mistook them for escaped convicts and alerted _____ authorities.

The man, identified only as Mr Wang, had returned to Shanghai recently to visit _____ girlfriend.

He had been studying in _____ Japan for two years, *Shanghai Morning Post* reported.

On _____ Wednesday night, _____ couple decided to travel to Hangzhou, the capital of Zhejiang province.

To show _____ deep love for her, he produced _____ pair of handcuffs and locked _____ wrists together, explaining to her that this was currently _____ most popular way of expressing love in Japan.

As they walked _____ hand in hand — literally — in _____ city, _____ tourist, thinking that they were _____ escaped convicts, reported them to _____ policeman.

Text 3

_____ pet shop in Hong Kong is renting out _____ puppies in _____ effort to find _____ "solution to _____ problem of dogs being dumped by _____ owners" (*South China Morning Post*, August 29).

I am opposed to _____ horrible rental scheme, because it will not be good for _____ mental health of _____ puppies.

Imagine having _____ human baby on rental. _____ child would be traumatized and grow up without any sense of having _____ permanent identity. _____ puppies that are rented out will be troubled in _____ own canine way. As they grow up they may find it difficult to respond to _____ humans. It may be good for _____ pet shop's business, but _____ proprietor should think about how it will affect _____ dogs mentally.

Text 4

Premier Zhu Rongji is more popular than President Jiang Zemin among _____ young Hong Kong people, _____ survey found yesterday — but late leaders Deng Xiaoping and Mao Zedong are admired even more.

Mr Zhu ranked fourth in _____ list of best leaders, with 23 votes, while Mr Jiang came 12th with only eight votes.

_____ survey of 502 people was conducted by _____ Hong Kong Federation of Youth Groups.

Topping _____ list was Sun Yat-sen, founder of _____ modern China, followed by Deng Xiaoping and Mao.

Former US president Bill Clinton, at seventh, was _____ highest-ranking foreign leader.

_____ phone survey was carried out _____ last month and respondents were aged 15 to 34.

Democratic Party legislator Cheung Man-kwong said that Mr Zhu had successfully established _____ good image among _____ Hong Kong public with _____ determination to fight corruption on _____ mainland.

"It seems that Zhu is _____ type of leader Hong Kong people would accept," he said.

Interviewees were also asked to list _____ qualities needed most by _____ good leader.

_____ integrity was ranked top, followed by _____ credibility, management skills and ability to communicate well.

Text 5

Fixed-line phone networks were flooded with 26 million calls in _____ hour on Wednesday after _____ Observatory announced just before _____ midday that _____ No. 8 typhoon signal would be hoisted.
_____ flood of calls between midday and 1 pm was up to six times _____ capacity of _____ networks, which between them can handle only about four million calls an hour, _____ Office of the Telecommunications Authority (Ofta) said.
_____ mobile networks, which have _____ similar combined capacity, were flooded with 14 million calls in _____ same hour. There are four fixed-line operators and six mobile phone networks in _____ territory. Ofta secretary-general Anthony Wong Sei-kei defended the networks, saying all remained functioning and none crashed. "_____ reason people could not get through was because all the networks were overloaded," he said.

3

Tense and Finiteness

Verb Forms

If you look at a typical piece of writing by an average student, you are bound to notice a lot of errors which have to do with the forms of **verbs**. Why is it so difficult to learn to use verbs correctly in English?

Let's start by looking at Chinese. Take any verb — say, the verb *chi* (吃 'eat').

 QUESTION 1

How many different forms does the Chinese verb *chi* (吃) have?

Answer:

In Chinese, a verb has only *one* form. *Chi* is always *chi* — no matter who, no matter when, no matter how. Now take the English verb *eat*.

QUESTION 2

Can you list all the different forms of the verb *eat*?

```
Answer:


```

You should have at least five: *eat, eats, eating, ate, eaten*. You might have an additional form, the infinitive *to eat* (we'll explain in the Notes and Answer Key section why this may be necessary). Just to make it easier for us to refer to them from now on, let's give each of them a label. We'll use the verbs *eat* and *talk* for illustration:

	Verb Form	**Label**
(i)	*eat, talk*	present tense (general)
(ii)	*eats, talks*	present tense (3rd person singular)
(iii)	*ate, talked*	past tense
(iv)	*eating, talking*	present participle
(v)	*eaten, talked*	past participle
(vi)	*(to) eat, (to) talk*	infinitive

 QUESTION 3

Give the six forms of the following verbs:

	wash	break	run	hear
Present tense (general)	_____	_____	_____	_____
Present tense (3rd per. sing.)	_____	_____	_____	_____
Past tense	_____	_____	_____	_____
Present participle	_____	_____	_____	_____
Past participle	_____	_____	_____	_____
Infinitive	_____	_____	_____	_____

Most verbs in English are like *talk* and *wash*, in having '**regular**' past tense and past participle forms, which are formed by attaching the suffix — *ed* to the verb, as in *talk, talked* (past tense), *talked* (past participle).

1. They *talk* too much.
2. They *talked* too much yesterday.
3. They have *talked* too much already.

[NB: For an explanation why we treat *talked* in (3) as past participle rather than past tense, see the Notes section for this unit.] In contrast, a certain number of verbs — especially among the more 'basic' verbs like *eat, see, run*, etc. — are '**irregular**', because they form the past tense and past participle in other ways than by adding *-ed*, as in *eat, ate, eaten; see, saw, seen; run, ran, run*, etc.

4. They *eat* too much.
5. They *ate* too much yesterday.
6. They have *eaten* too much already.

For such verbs, you'll just have to memorize their irregular forms.

Tense

Merely knowing the **forms** of verbs is a relatively trivial matter — if in doubt, just look it up in a dictionary. What is less easy and much more important is to learn to use these different forms of verbs properly in their various **functions**.

One of the most important functions of verb forms is to show **tense**. Tense is one of the most noticeable differences between English and Chinese grammar. As you know, Chinese has no tense. For example, the verb '住' (live) in sentence 7 is neither in the present nor the past tense:

7. 他住在大埔 ('he live in Taipo')

This does not, of course, mean that Chinese has no way of indicating time. In Chinese, you can indicate the time frame by using such phrases as 'now' (現在), 'before' (以前), 'after' (以後), 'already' (已經), 'yesterday' (昨天), etc. and other devices like **aspect**, which we'll not go into here, as in:

8. 'He *now* live in Taipo' (他<u>現在</u>住在大埔)
9. 'He *before* live in Taipo' (他<u>以前</u>住在大埔)

The big difference between English and Chinese is this:

- In English, a time frame — 'past' or 'present' — is *built into* the grammar of verbs, rather than just added on as extra words.

English grammar forces us to commit the main verb of a sentence to either the **present** or **past tense**. The English equivalents of sentences 8–9 are thus:

10. He *lives* in Taipo.
11. He *lived* in Taipo.

(If we like, we can add 'now' or 'in the past' to these sentences for extra emphasis, but they are not necessary in English, as they are in Chinese, to distinguish present and past.)

Which of the six forms of a verb are used to indicate tense? Three of them, namely:

Present tense (general)	: *eat, talk*
Present tense (3rd per. sing.)	: *eats, talks*
Past tense	: *ate, talked*

The above three forms are thus called **tensed** or '**finite**' forms. 'Finite' suggests 'limited'. Take any verb from a dictionary — e.g. the verb *eat*, which means 'to consume food'. In the 'infinitive' form, not marked for tense, the verb only stands for a *type* of action, rather than any individual occurrence of that action.

Do you recall the discussion on nouns in Unit 2? A noun on its own, like 'book', stands only for a *type* of object, and does not refer to any individual book in the world. But if we mark it with a **determiner** like *the, this, my* etc., then it refers not just to any book, but to a particular book.

Thus, there's something in common in the grammar of nouns and verbs in English. In order for a verb to refer to an actual occurrence of an action, or a noun to refer to an actual object, it has to be 'limited' in some way, to a particular time (present or past), or a particular entity (this or that object). This is basically what '**finite**' means.

Thus, a verb which is marked for tense is said to be 'finite' because the tense *limits* the reference of the verb to some time frame, present or past. For example:

10. He *lives* in Taipo.
    (*lives* = limited to occurrence in the **present** time frame, and with a **singular** subject.)
11. He *lived* in Taipo.
    (*lived* = limited to occurrence in the **past** time frame.)

Compare and contrast these with the **non-finite** (i.e. without tense) forms, e.g. *to live, living*:

12. *Living* in Taipo can be hazardous to your health.
13. *To live* in Suzhou is heaven.

Unlike the finite forms *lives* and *lived*, the non-finite forms *living* and *to live* do not refer to any actual occurrence of the act of 'living', and can refer to any time and anybody.

The first important point to remember about the use of tenses in English is this:

- **The main verb of a sentence must be finite (i.e. marked for tense)**

Here are some exercises to give you more practice in the use of finite verb forms.

Tense and Finiteness   45

 QUESTION 4

The underlined verbs in the following sentences are finite (i.e. marked for tense). Explain in what sense each verb is 'finite' — i.e. limited to what time frame and (if possible) what kind of subject?

1. He <u>lived</u> in Hong Kong when he <u>was</u> a child. Now he <u>lives</u> in Singapore.
2. In 1950, a domestic maid <u>earned</u> about $50 a month; now she <u>earns</u> $3,600.
3. When he <u>arrived</u> home last night, he <u>found</u> the door broken, so he <u>called</u> the police.
4. Whenever he <u>has</u> time, he <u>swims</u> and <u>jogs</u> to stay in shape.
5. Though the last plane <u>has</u> left, many people <u>are</u> still waiting for a flight out.
6. He <u>did</u> not report for work yesterday as he <u>was</u> not feeling well.

Answer:

1.

2.

3.

4.

5.

6.

 QUESTION 5

A number of verbs with all their different forms are given below. In each of the following sentences, fill in the blank with the *correct form* of any of the verbs given. [NB: In some cases more than one answer is possible.]

VERBS:
eat, eats, eating, ate, eaten, to eat
see, sees, seeing, saw, seen, to see
live, lives, living, lived, to live
write, writes, writing, wrote, written, to write
break, breaks, breaking, broke, broken, to break
hear, hears, hearing, heard, to hear

1. He _____ the new James Bond movie last week.
2. She _____ letters to her parents very often.
3. He _____ the door with his hands.
4. Tom _____ the news on the radio.
5. He _____ nothing but boiled vegetables.
6. He _____ in Repulse Bay, but his wife _____ in Ma On Shan.

You will find that *only* **finite** forms of verbs can occur in the blanks in the above sentences. All these slots are for the main verb of the sentence.

QUESTION 6

The following sentences are taken from students' writings. Correct the errors in the **tense** of the verbs.

1. Half of the respondents being neutral with that question.

2. Millions of years ago, some of the lands become seas, and some becomes rivers.

3. The vegetation was covered by a layer of mud which consist of sand and small rocks.

4. I went to the park and watch the kids play football.

Verb Groups

Quite often, verbs in English occur in *groups* rather than singly. Each group consists of a **main verb**, which is always at the *end* of the group, preceded by one or more **auxiliary verbs** ('helping verbs'), as in 'He *could have been crying*'. Look at the sentences below (14–24). Each of them contains a verb group (underlined for you). (Notice that, as in 23–24, the verb group need not be continuous, but can be 'split up' by other words.)

Tense and Finiteness   47

14. He <u>is washing</u> his dog.
15. He <u>was washing</u> his dog at that time.
16. He <u>has taken</u> his dog for a walk.
17. He <u>had taken</u> his dog for a walk when I called.
18. He <u>can jump</u> over this fence easily.
19. He <u>could jump</u> over this fence when he was slimmer.
20. He <u>should have taken</u> his job more seriously.
21. He <u>has been arrested</u> many times.
22. He <u>had been waiting</u> for two hours when she finally arrived.
23. He <u>did</u> not <u>say</u> that he was unhappy.
24. <u>Did</u> he <u>say</u> that he was unhappy?

QUESTION 7

Look at sentences 14–24 above. Are *all* the verbs in each verb group marked individually for tense? If not, circle the verb which is marked for tense (present or past). Can you make a simple generalization about which verb in a verb group is marked for tense in all cases?

Answer:

I think the answer should not be difficult to find:

- **In a finite verb group, only the *first* verb is marked for tense**

So remember this: If the main verb occurs alone (without any auxiliary verbs), it is marked for tense (e.g. 'He ***stopped***'). But if we have a verb group instead of a single verb, then it is the very *first* verb in the group which is marked for tense, and not the main verb or any other verb in the group. In the following examples, the verb groups are enclosed in brackets. Notice that it is always the first verb in the group which is marked for tense, and all the other verbs are in either the bare form or some present or past participle form:

He [*could* not stop] in time.
He [*would* stop] if you asked him.
He [*was* sleeping] in the middle of my lecture.
He [*has* been sleeping] a lot in class lately.

QUESTION 8

Some (but not all) of the verbs in the following sentences are in the wrong form. Identify and correct these errors:

1. Would Kevin stopped seeing his friends?
2. She can't tolerated such an unreliable relationship.
3. More than 50% did not agreed with that.
4. She can't be bothered with all these details.
5. He did not wash the dishes last night.
6. He always playing in the field.
7. The window broken by someone yesterday.
8. When I phoned him last night, he having a shower.

Answer:

QUESTION 9

Fill in the blank in each of the following sentences with the correct form of the verb in brackets. Remember, if the verb belongs to a verb group, then only the first verb in the group can be marked for tense.

1. Though I asked him many times, he would not _____ (tell) me the answer.
2. When the bill came, he suddenly realized that he did not _____ (have) enough money.

3. Do you think he should _____ (apologize) for what he said?
4. How could he possibly _____ (know) what we were planning?
5. I did not deliberately _____ (step) on your toes.
6. Whenever it rains, the temperature always _____ (drop).
7. When the enemy advanced, they _____ (retreat), and when the enemy retreated, they _____ (advance).
8. His wife told him to _____ (buy) a watermelon, but he _____ (buy) a durian instead.
9. Though he is very rich, he never _____ (show) it.
10. Though he was poor, he _____ (pretend) to be rich.

Present Tense

To recapitulate, the main verb of a sentence in English must be **finite**, i.e. marked for **tense**. There are three tensed forms:

Present tense (general):	*sing, dance*	'They sing and dance for a living'
Present tense (3rd per. sing.):	*sings, dances*	'He sings and dances for a living'
Past tense:	*sang, danced*	'He sang and danced for a living'

We will discuss the non-finite forms — e.g. *singing, sung, (to) sing* — in later units (4 and 9), on 'auxiliaries' and 'non-finite clauses' respectively.

Here, we'll go into the use of the tenses in English. The names '**present**' **tense** and '**past**' **tense** do have an obvious meaning — *generally*, verbs in the present tense do refer to present occurrences or states, and verbs in the past tense to past occurrences or states. But these are just generalizations, and verbs in the present tense especially have a much wider range of uses beyond just referring to present time. We'll try to work them out in the following exercises.

 ## QUESTION 10

The verbs in the following sentences are in the present tense ('simple present tense'). What time frame do they actually refer to — e.g. to the present moment (i.e. the moment of speaking), or what? [Hint: It may be helpful to take 1–4 separately from 5–8.]

1. He *plays* tennis every day.
2. He *plays* tennis only once a year.
3. The boy usually *delivers* the paper early, but this morning he's late.
4. The boy seldom *delivers* the paper on time.
5. She *lives* here, but right now she is visiting her parents in Beijing.

6. I *know* six different languages.
7. Shark fin *costs* more than crab meat.
8. He *owns* half the buildings in this town.

Answer:

 QUESTION 11

In Question 10, you've seen how the present tense can be used to refer to certain time frames which do not necessarily coincide with the present moment. In the following sentences, the present tense is used to indicate yet another time frame. Can you describe what it is?

1. The earth *revolves* round the sun, and the moon *revolves* round the earth.
2. Pure water *boils* at 100 degrees Celsius at sea level.
3. Gold *weighs* more than silver.
4. Cows *eat* grass, but monkeys *prefer* bananas.

Answer:

QUESTION 12

Here are some more sentences where the verbs are in the present tense. What time frame do they actually refer to, and is it different from questions 10–11?

1. The plane *leaves* early tomorrow morning.
2. The first semester *ends* on December 18.
3. The first one to move, *dies*.
4. The fasting month *begins* next week.

Answer:

In Questions 10–12, we looked at some uses of the 'simple' Present Tense which do not really refer to occurrences at precisely the present moment (i.e. the moment of speaking). We begin to wonder, does the so-called simple Present Tense ever refer to something happening right at the present moment? How about the sentences in Question 13?

 QUESTION 13

What time frame do you think we're looking at in the following sentences?

1. I *resign*!
2. I hereby *sentence* you to life imprisonment.
3. I *declare* this meeting open.
4. [TV Commentator:] Ronaldo *passes* the ball to Ronaldino, but Alberto *intercepts* and *passes* it to Albertino.

Answer:

The above use of the simple Present Tense is rather limited. In the next unit, we'll see how the Present Tense can be combined with the Progressive Aspect to refer in general to events actually occurring at the present moment.

Past Tense

While the present tense has a broad range of uses (as you'll have noticed from the above exercises), the **past tense** does actually refer to past time in the great majority of cases. So we need not do any exercises on this. Most mistakes are due to students' neglecting to use the past tense, rather than to any misunderstanding. So, just be more careful!

There are, however, a few 'specialized' uses of the past tense which do not really have anything to do with past time. The most important of these has to do with **conditional** ('if ... then') sentences. There are three main types of conditionals, some involving and some not involving the past tense:

(i) If it *rains*, we *will* cancel the game. [present tense]
(ii) If it *rained*, we *would* cancel the game. [past tense]
(iii) If it *had rained*, we *would have cancelled* the game. [past perfect]

From these examples alone, without a context, it would be hard to guess what the differences are. The following exercise will help.

 QUESTION 14

Analyse the following examples, where the verbs in the conditional sentences are underlined. You will find examples of all the three forms given in (i–iii) above. Do not think of any differences in time (there are none). Rather, try to relate the three different verb forms to this question: *how likely* and *how real* is the situation we're talking about in this sentence?

1. I haven't heard from him yet. If I <u>hear</u> anything, I <u>will let</u> you know immediately.
2. I honestly don't know the answer. If I <u>knew</u>, I <u>would tell</u> you right now.
3. He didn't know at that time that she was a divorcee. If he <u>had known</u>, he <u>would not have proposed</u> to her.
4. I'll have to check my bank balance. If I <u>have</u> enough money, I <u>will</u> join the tour.
5. If I <u>had</u> a million dollars, I <u>would</u> donate it to my university. But I don't think I'll ever have that much money.
6. I regret that I did not donate my winnings to charity. If I <u>had done</u> that, I <u>would have avoided</u> having to pay so much tax.
7. If you <u>call</u> after 9 tonight, I <u>will</u> be home. I'm not so sure about tomorrow night though.
8. No, he did not call last night. If he <u>had called</u>, I <u>would have given</u> him a scolding.
9. No, I don't think he's going to call. But even if he <u>called</u>, I <u>would not answer</u> the phone anyway.

The differences between the three forms, in terms of likelihood or reality, are:

Present Tense:

Past Tense:

Past Perfect:

QUESTION 15

In items 1–3 below, all three forms of the conditional (present tense, past tense, past perfect) are given and underlined. Circle the form which you think is the most *appropriate* in this particular situation. In 4–6, fill in the blank with the most suitable form of the verb in brackets.

1. Luckily it stopped raining two days ago. If the rain <u>does not stop/did not stop/had not stopped</u>, the town <u>will be flooded/would be flooded/would have been flooded</u>.
2. I'm going to the bookstore this afternoon. If I <u>find/found/had found</u> the book, I <u>will get/would get/would have got</u> it for you.
3. If I <u>am/were/had been</u> your father, I <u>will spank/would spank/would have spanked</u> you, but I'm only your teacher.
4. The police are out looking for the terrorist. If they _____ (find) him, they _____ (shoot) him on sight.
5. The police surrounded the terrorists' hideout but failed to catch anyone. If they _____ (catch) some of the terrorists, the police chief _____ (be) very proud of them.
6. Unfortunately, he doesn't exercise or play any sports. If he _____ (do), he _____ (not be) as fat as he is now.

Understanding English Grammar

Additional Exercises

Though the concept of tense is not found in Chinese, it is not really that difficult a concept to understand. What is more difficult is to remember to use it, for English requires the main verb of a sentence to be finite (or tensed). Here are a few more exercises on tense for you.

EXERCISE 1

Underline all the verbs in the following text, and identify each of them as either **finite** or **non-finite**. [Treat a whole verb group as one verb.] If the verb is finite, say whether it is in the present or past tense.

> There is something about lying on your back in a hospital bed with half a dozen needles poking out of your skin that makes you really ponder your health, and how to maintain it.
>   The sound of the old man in the next bed snoring loudly is testament to just how relaxing acupuncture really can be. But being the youngest patient in the clinic by at least two generations did make me wonder whether acupuncture and its associated traditional therapies are strictly for the old.

EXERCISE 2

In each of the following texts, fill in the blanks with the appropriate forms of the verbs in brackets:

Text 1

A passenger _____ (tell) yesterday of frightening scenes aboard the holiday cruise ship *SuperStar Leo* when it _____ (run) into severe tropical storm Hagupit on Wednesday, forcing it to _____ (change) course and _____ (return) to Hong Kong a day late.

   Passengers _____ (be) slammed against walls, tables _____ (overturn) and luggage _____ (fall) from overhead lockers, the passenger said.

   The vessel's operator, *Star Cruises*, _____ (confirm) the day-long delay _____ (be) caused by the closure of Hong Kong harbour, which _____ (force) *Leo* to _____ (seek) shelter near Dangan Island, about 30 km south of Tsing Yi in mainland waters. However, the company _____ (deny) that anyone _____ (have) been injured.

   The passenger said weather conditions _____ (deteriorate) quickly after 1 pm on Wednesday and the ship _____ (be) rocked heavily until after 5 pm. *Leo*

_____ (be) scheduled to return to Ocean Terminal at 4 pm on Wednesday but eventually _____ (return) to Hong Kong at 10 am on Thursday.

Text 2

Father Franco Mella _____ (put) even more weight behind the right-of-abode seekers after his return from a four-month visit home to Italy — where he _____ (pile) on 10 kg.

The 53-year-old, who _____ (begin) a hunger strike next Monday to promote the right-of-abode cause, _____ (say) the homemade pasta, pizza and salami served up by his 79-year-old mother _____ (be) behind his expanded waistline.

The priest, who now _____ (weigh) about 95 kg, _____ (point) out that he _____ (lose) about 10 kg when he _____ (stage) a 10-day hunger strike with the abode seekers last April before returning to his home in Italy.

"When my mother first _____ (see) me, she _____ (ask) me never to fast again. But when she later _____ (see) me becoming fatter and fatter, she _____ (say): 'You better go back to Hong Kong'," Father Mella said.

4

Auxiliary Verbs and Aspect

Introduction

In Unit 3, you saw that a verb in English is not always used alone, but often together with one or more **auxiliary verbs** (or 'auxiliaries' for short) to form a **verb group.** In this unit, we'll explore the most important grammatical functions that are associated with the use of auxiliaries.

There are two broad types of auxiliaries in English: **primary auxiliaries** and **modal auxiliaries.** We will focus on the primary auxiliaries here, as they are much harder to learn, and are much more different from Chinese, than the modal auxiliaries. The primary auxiliaries in English are *be, have,* and *do*. You should not confuse these auxiliaries with the **main verbs** below:

1. My neighbour *is* rich.
2. He *has* a Rolls Royce.
3. He always *does* his work after dinner.

The verbs *be, have* and *do* in the above sentences are main verbs and are used on their own, but what we're dealing with in this unit are the uses of these verbs as **auxiliaries**, as in:

4. My neighbour *is walking* his dog.
5. He *has bought* a Jack Russell.
6. The dog *does* not *bark* at strangers.

The Auxiliary *be* and the Progressive Aspect

As an auxiliary, *be* has two main uses. The first is to mark **progressive aspect**. [NB: The 'progressive aspect' is also known as 'continuous tense' (is a misleading term which we'll avoid here).] The progressive aspect is marked by the auxiliary *be* + the **present participle** form of the main verb, for example:

7. He <u>is/was dancing</u> with his partner.
8. They <u>are/were singing</u> the song 'Changing Partners'.

If *be* is the first verb of the verb group, it will be marked for either present or past tense, as in the above examples.

The form itself is quite simple. It is much more important to understand the uses of the progressive aspect. The following questions will help you to work them out.

 QUESTION 1

The following sentences have verbs in the present tense with or without progressive aspect. By comparing the two, can you figure out the main use of the progressive aspect?

1. He usually *plays* tennis on weekends, but not today.
2. No, he's not in his office right now. He *is playing* tennis at the club.
3. He *washes* his car every day.
4. He *is washing* his car now, but he should be back in a few minutes.
5. She *waits* for her children at the bus stop after school each day.
6. She *is waiting* for you at the bus stop, so better hurry now!
7. I *feel* very satisfied with the way I've lived my life.
8. I *am feeling* sick. I've got to lie down.

Answer:
The progressive aspect is used to indicate:

Please check your answers before proceeding to the next question.

QUESTION 2

The examples in Question 1 show only the simplest use of the progressive aspect. The following data may look similar, but if you think about it, they do not show exactly the same use of the progressive aspect as in Question 1. What similarities and differences do you notice between them?

1. She *writes* romantic novels for a hobby.
2. She *is writing* a book on Leslie Cheung at the moment. It'll probably be finished by the end of the year.
3. My brother *lives* with my parents.
4. My brother *is living* with my parents these days, but he'll move into his new apartment when it's ready.
5. He normally *plays* villains and psychopaths in his movies, but he *is* now *playing* good guys for a change.

Answer:

 QUESTION 3

How do you think the progressive aspect is used in the following examples?

1. I *am leaving* for London this weekend.
2. He *is moving* to the Peak next month.
3. Beijing *is hosting* the Olympic Games in 2008.
4. What *are* you *doing* tomorrow evening?
5. When *are* you *starting* your new job?

Answer:

You have seen three of the most important uses of the progressive aspect. What you should also know about the progressive aspect is that it *cannot* be used with *all* verbs in English.

 QUESTION 4

Which of the following verbs are wrongly used in the progressive aspect?

1. I *am knowing* five languages.
2. He *is having* a house and a car.
3. She *is liking* classical music.
4. This book *is belonging to me*.
5. I *am understanding* your problem.
6. They *are thinking* about the problem.

Answer:
The progressive aspect is wrongly used in:

Can you explain why most of the above verbs cannot be used in the progressive aspect? Before you do that, you may want to compare English with Chinese. Chinese expresses the progressive aspect by attaching the progressive 'marker' *zai* (在) before the verb, e.g. *ta zai kan shu* (他在看書 'He's reading a book'). In Chinese, too, there are certain verbs that you cannot attach *zai* to.

Auxiliary Verbs and Aspect   61

 QUESTION 5

Give the Chinese equivalents of the sentences in Question 4. [NB: If you need to use Cantonese, the Cantonese progressive marker is *gen* (緊), which you attach after the verb, e.g. *koi tai gen xu* (佢睇緊書 'He's reading a book').] Which Chinese verbs cannot take the progressive marker? Do you notice any similarities with English?

Answer:

You will no doubt discover that, by and large, *similar verbs* in English and Chinese cannot take the progressive aspect marker! Is this a coincidence?

 QUESTION 6

Can you think of an explanation why certain types of verbs both in English and Chinese cannot take the progressive aspect? This may not be a simple question, so we'll give you a clue. First, think of what the progressive aspect does (refer to Questions 1 and 2 in particular); then, think of the nature of the 'activity' or 'state' that the verbs in Question 4 stand for. Is there a clash between these activities or states and the meaning of the progressive aspect? (Don't just think of 'mental' vs. 'physical' alone, as *think* and *understand* are both mental, and yet the latter cannot take the progressive aspect.) A common-sense explanation would be enough.

Answer:

Now let's try to sum up what we have learnt from Questions 1–6 about the progressive aspect in English. Questions 1 and 2 have brought out the central uses of the progressive aspect, namely:

- **The progressive aspect typically indicates an ongoing and unfinished activity, or a temporary state.**

Thus, sentence 4 in Question 1, 'He is washing his car now', indicates that the activity of washing his car is going on and unfinished at the moment of speaking, and that it is something which is temporary and not permanent (that is, his washing of the car will come to an end some time). The examples in Question 2 emphasize the temporariness. For example, 'My brother is living with my parents these days' implies that this is a temporary arrangement, not a permanent one.

With the above characterization in mind, it makes sense that certain states which are not normally temporary but are (more or less) permanent, such as *to know, like, understand,* etc. do not fit well with the progressive aspect. (Note that, unlike *understand*, *think* [in the sense of using your mind] is a temporary activity, and hence can take the progressive aspect.) We can make the following generalization:

- **Verbs that indicate non-temporary or permanent states (e.g. *know* or *understand*) cannot be used with the progressive aspect.**

 ## QUESTION 7

In the following sentences, can you explain why what looks like the same verb (e.g. *have*) can be ungrammatical (*) in one sentence but grammatical in another when used with the progressive aspect? (Clue: Do these two uses of the same verb have the same meaning?)

1. * He *is having* a sports car.
2. He *is having* his dinner.
3. * He *is seeing* the picture on the wall.
4. The doctor *is seeing* his patients in the surgery.
5. * This book *is costing* $100.
6. I must resign from the club. It *is costing* me too much.

Answer:

QUESTION 8

So far we have been using the progressive aspect in combination with the present tense — or 'present progressive' for short. The following are some examples where it is combined with the past tense ('past progressive'). What do you think the past progressive indicates?

1. When I rang last night, he *was having* his shower.
2. I *was driving* to Hong Kong island when the typhoon struck.
3. Two hours after the football match, the fans *were* still *hanging* around.
4. What *was* the burglar *doing* when the police arrived? He *was trying* to climb over the fence.
5. When the earthquake struck, some people *were rushing* into buildings while others *were rushing* out of them.

Answer:

As we have seen in the first part of this unit, the first function of the auxiliary *be* is to indicate progressive aspect. The second important function is to indicate **passive voice**, as in: 'The windows *were smashed* by the typhoon'. We will deal with this in Unit 5.
One final note: Some students use *be* unnecessarily, e.g.

1. * I *am agree* with you.
2. * I *am* strongly *recommend* this book to all of you.
3. * We *were asked* 30 chief executives about what is necessary.

 QUESTION 9

What do you think the students were trying to say in sentences 1–3 above? Is there a difference in their saying 'I *am* agree with you' and the normal 'I agree with you'? Discuss this with your classmates and teacher.

Since the use of *be* in sentences like 1–3 above is ungrammatical, take care to avoid using it this way. If you think the writer was trying to add emphasis by using *be,* the proper way is to use *do* ('I do agree with you', etc.)

The Auxiliary *have* and the Perfect Aspect

Present perfect

The auxiliary *have* has one main function: i.e. to mark the **perfect aspect**, e.g. 'I *have eaten* already'. There's that word again, 'aspect'. Maybe we should pause here to ask what 'aspect' means in general.

Aspect has to do with how a situation (an event or a state) is *viewed*. As you know, a situation can be seen from a number of different 'viewpoints'. For example, you can look at it as something going on at some point of time (such as right now). The **progressive** aspect does that. 'He's dancing on the table' means the activity of dancing is happening right now (at the moment of speaking). What we see is only what's going on at this moment, and does not include the beginning or end of that activity. The dancing started before you say this sentence, and will go on after you've said it.

Now, what 'viewpoint' is connected with the **perfect aspect**?

 QUESTION **10**

The following sentences contain verbs in the present tense and perfect aspect (or 'present perfect' for short). In these sentences, what is the viewpoint from which we are looking at the underlined event (e.g. from the beginning, middle, end, or what)?

1. I <u>have finished</u> my homework, so I can sit back and enjoy a video now.
2. You <u>have eaten</u> two pizzas already — do you really want more?
3. He <u>has gone</u> to Japan, and won't be back till next week.
4. I <u>have applied</u> for ten jobs, but so far I <u>have received</u> only two replies.
5. She <u>has married</u> and <u>divorced</u> eight times already, and is now working on husband No. 9.

Answer:

As you may have concluded above, the perfect aspect views an event from the *end-point*, as something that is *completed*. The combination of **present tense** *and* **perfect aspect** (as in sentences 1–5 above) implies that something is completed *before the present moment*. So, 'I have finished my homework' means that, before the present moment (the moment of speaking), the homework was completed, and therefore I am free to enjoy myself now.

Past perfect

What about the combination of **past tense** and perfect aspect (the 'past perfect')? Question 11 below will help you think about how it should be used.

 QUESTION 11

Look at the way the past perfect (underlined) is used in the following sentences. When did the event referred to in the past perfect take place?

1. By the time I arrived at the airport, the plane had left.
2. By 1960, the population of Hong Kong had reached 3 million, and by 1990, it had exceeded 6 million.
3. Luckily for him, by the time he retired, his children had all grown up.
4. When he reached home, he found his house in a mess. Someone had broken all the windows. They had even smashed the flowerpots.

Answer:

As the name itself suggests, the use of the 'past perfect' implies that something was completed *before some other point of time in the past*. This is an important point. The past perfect is often misused by students, who treat it as if it were the same as the simple past tense, but it is not.

 **QUESTION 12**

In the following pairs of sentences a–b, the past perfect is used correctly in one but wrongly in the other. Identify where the past perfect is wrongly used, and explain why it is wrong:

(1a) He *had moved* to his new home yesterday.
(1b) He *had moved* to his new home by the time he got married.

(2a) By the end of the War the Americans *had dropped* two atom bombs on Japan.
(2b) In August 1945 the Americans *had dropped* two atom bombs on Japan.

 QUESTION 13

Fill in the blanks in the following passages with the correct forms of the verbs in brackets:

1. After more than 150 years of colonial rule, Hong Kong reverted to China on July 1, 1997. By that time, it _____ (grow) from a barren rock to one of the most modern and prosperous cities in the world, and the population _____ (increase) from a few hundred to six million. After 1997, many of the people who _____ (migrate) overseas earlier _____ (begin) to return, as they _____ (find) that things were not so bad after all.

2. Recently, I returned to my old neighbourhood to look for my childhood friend. I found that she _____ (move) out long ago. Some neighbours told me that she _____ (marry) a rich old man from America, but others said that she _____ (join) the sisterhood and _____ (go) to serve in India. Someone even said that she _____ (die). I hope that I can find her again some day.

Present perfect again

Now let's go back to the present perfect, which (as we've seen) refers to events completed before the present moment. A natural question to ask at this point is this: if both the **simple past tense** and the **present perfect** refer to events which were completed before the present — e.g. 'I wrote a letter' and 'I have written a letter' — then what is the difference?

 QUESTION 14

Compare the sentences below, where the verb is used either in the past tense or the present perfect. [NB: Those marked with * are unacceptable.] Can you explain why some are grammatical and some are not, and describe the differences between how the past tense and present perfect should be used?

1. His forefathers *arrived* in this country in 1900.
2. * His forefathers *have arrived* in this country in 1900.
3. The train *left* two minutes ago.
4. * The train *has left* two minutes ago.
5. The train *has* just *left*.
6. He *has written* many books since 1989.
7. * He *wrote* many books since 1989.
8. Until now, I *have* not *heard* from him.
9. * Until now, I *did* not *hear* from him.

Answer:

Apart from the above differences, some people think that the present perfect is used for very recent events, and the past tense for events further back. Even if this is a typical interpretation, is it *necessarily* true? Consider the following sentences, which are perfectly normal:

1. I *saw* him just now. (This happened a few minutes ago.)
2. I *have seen* this film before. (The film is *Gone with the Wind* and you actually saw it many years ago.)

You will see that 'recentness' is not really the crucial point here. Then what is?

 QUESTION 15

There are some fine differences between the sentences in the past tense and present perfect below. Can you tell which ones are more appropriate and which ones less appropriate? Can you explain why?

1. A: Can we start the party now? B: Sure, my parents *have left*.
2. A: Can we start the party now? B: Sure, my parents *left*.

3. The guests *have arrived*. Bring out the food.
4. The guests *arrived*. Bring out the food.
5. A: Would you like to join us for dinner? B: No thank you, I *have eaten*.
6. A: Would you like to join us for dinner? B: No thank you, I *ate*.
7. Can you give me a lift home? The last bus *has left*.
8. Can you give me a lift home? The last bus *left*.

Answer:

Perfect + progressive aspect

English grammar allows us to combine the perfect and progressive aspects within the same verb group, for example, 'I *have been living* here for ten years'. This may sound awfully complicated, but the following exercise should help you understand it a little better.

 QUESTION 16

In the following sentences, you will find verb groups which are either in the present perfect or the present perfect progressive. From the contexts provided in these sentences, can you figure out the difference between the two?

1. I *have written* a novel. It was hard work and I am glad it's finished at last.
2. I *have been writing* a novel. It's been two years since I started it, and I have no idea when I'll be able to finish it.
3. I *have read* the exam scripts. There were no failures.
4. I *have been reading* the exam scripts. I think I should be able to finish by tomorrow evening.
5. He *has helped* me before, and I'm sure he'll help me again.
6. He *has been helping* me in his spare time, but I don't think he can go on helping me much longer.

Answer:

The Auxiliary *do*

Do has been called a 'dummy' auxiliary. Do you know why?

 QUESTION 17

From the following examples, can you explain the uses of the auxiliary *do?*

1. I know where he lives.
2. I *do* not know where he lives.
3. *Do* you know where he lives?
4. Yes, I *do*.
5. He climbed Mount Everest alone.
6. *Did* he climb Mount Everest alone?
7. He *did* not climb Mount Everest alone.
8. Why *did* he climb Mount Everest alone?
9. When *did* he climb Mount Everest?

Answer:

A common error is to leave out the auxiliary *do* when it's needed, for example:

1. Why ^ they *go* to the center of the earth?
2. She thinks he ^ *not know*.

Such errors are not surprising for Chinese students, because in Chinese the above sentences would be perfectly correct, since Chinese does not have any auxiliaries like *do*.

Other than the above uses, *do* is also used for emphasis: 'I *do* believe that he is innocent'. But be careful — it should only be used occasionally, not regularly.

Additional Exercises

Fill in the blanks with the correct forms of the verbs in brackets:

Text 1

Global economic growth _____ (take) its toll on the environment, and Hong Kong's pollution is certainly the worst I _____ (see). The warning bells _____ (ring) and the air pollution index (API) readings keep increasing in Hong Kong. Strict policies and fines _____ (be put) in place, and it is well-known that the removal of lead from petrol and the use of energy-efficient technology can also greatly reduce the problems. But why _____ the situation not _____ (improve)? Can't the government do more to fight pollution?

It may be our fault. Many environmental measures _____ (be set), but only a few people support them. How can the air improve without our support?

The government should strictly punish people who throw rubbish on the streets or in the sea. Industries which _____ (pollute) our rivers and oceans must be hit with heavy fines.

Text 2

Under Article 23 of the Basic Law, Hong Kong is required to pass laws against acts of treason, secession, sedition, subversion and the theft of state secrets.

There _____ long _____ (be) concerns that the laws will restrict freedoms and be used to clamp down on dissent.

Officials both in Hong Kong and on the mainland _____ (seek) to play down the fears, while insisting that the time _____ (come) for the national security laws to be enacted. The government is expected to release a consultation paper soon, perhaps as early as next month.

Text 3

Since the downfall of former strongman Suharto in 1998, restrictions on Chinese culture _____ (begin) to lift.

Last year, President Megawati _____ (declare) Lunar New Year or Imlek as a national holiday, making it the first time that Chinese culture _____ (be recognized) officially since the 1965 ban.

Since 1999, Chinese Indonesians _____ (celebrate) Imlek openly, shopping malls _____ (be decked) out in red and gold lanterns every New Year, several Chinese-language newspapers _____ (hit) the streets, and Metro television station broadcasts the news several times a day in Putonghua.

But Hendrawan says, in practice, that many of the old laws discriminating against ethnic Chinese _____ (operate) still. Along with 100 other ethnic Chinese professionals, he _____ (meet) the president's husband, Taufiq Kiemas, last night, to demand equal rights for Chinese-Indonesians.

5

Transitivity and Passive Voice

Introduction

In this unit, we'll look at another important property of verbs, which seems to show some similarities between English and Chinese — and yet they are very different in some other ways.

 QUESTION 1

Here are some common verbs in English, each used in a sentence in a typical way. Based on how they are used here, can you divide them into two groups (let's call them Groups 'A' and 'B')? Can you give a reason for your choice?

1. He *slept*.
2. He *built* this house.
3. He *smiled*.
4. He *damaged* the vase.
5. He *died*.
6. He *scolded* the policeman.

'Group A' verbs:

'Group B' verbs:

It is almost certain that all of you will have divided the above sentences this way: 'Group A' verbs: 1, 3, 5; 'Group B': 2, 4, 6. What about the reason? You may have put it differently, but most of you will probably have said something like this: Group A verbs have **no objects,** and Group B verbs have **objects**.

 QUESTION 2

Here are some more sentences involving the same verbs as in 1–6 above. The way they are used this time, all the sentences are ungrammatical (as indicated by *). What do these additional data tell you about these verbs?

7. * He *slept* the floor.
8. * He *built*.
9. * He *smiled* the pretty girl.
10. * He *damaged*.
11. * He *died* his friend.
12. * He *scolded*.

Answer:

You will probably have arrived at the following conclusion: The first group of verbs (*sleep, smile, die*) **cannot** have objects, while the second group (*build, damage, scold*) **need** to have objects. That's why sentences 7–12 are ungrammatical.

 QUESTION 3

Think of three more verbs which are like Group A verbs (like *sleep* etc.), and another three verbs which are like Group B verbs (like *scold* etc.) Make a sentence with each of these new verbs.

Transitivity and Passive Voice   75

More Group A verbs:

More Group B verbs:

Unlike tense or number, the property that you've noticed about the verbs in this unit is not limited to English. Let's look at Chinese.

QUESTION 4

Give the Chinese equivalents of sentences 1–6 above. What similarities do you find between the Chinese and English verbs?

Answer:

You'll have discovered something quite interesting. And that is, in Chinese as well as in English, the same kinds of verbs (e.g. those in sentences 1, 3, 5) do not have objects, and the same kinds of verbs (e.g. those in 2, 4, 6) do.

Transitivity

From the Introduction, you will have got the idea that there are two types of verbs, in both English and Chinese, i.e.:

- Verbs that *cannot* take an **object** (e.g. *sleep, smile, die*) — we call them **intransitive verbs.**
- Verbs that *need* an **object** (e.g. *build, damage, scold*) — we call them **transitive verbs.**

What is an 'object'? A mere definition is not going to do you much good. The following questions will help you understand this concept better.

 QUESTION 5

In the following sentences, the verb (in bold print) is followed by an underlined phrase. Some of these underlined phrases are objects and some are not. Using what you may know about 'objects', can you identify those that are objects, and explain how you managed to distinguish them from non-objects?

1. He **sat** <u>on the floor</u>.
2. He **swept** <u>the floor</u>.
3. The teacher **shouted** <u>at the student</u>.
4. The teacher **praised** <u>the student</u>.
5. The baby **cried** <u>for milk</u>.
6. The baby **finished** <u>the milk</u>.
7. The boss **travelled** <u>by plane</u>.
8. The pilot **tested** <u>the plane</u>.

Answer:

One of the crucial points that you may have found from the above question is that an object is normally a **noun phrase** (like 'the floor'), rather than a **prepositional phrase** (i.e. a **preposition** followed by a noun phrase, like 'on the floor'). That is an important first step.

You can also discover another important property of the object by this simple test. Try to insert a word or phrase — such as 'patiently', 'loudly', 'for a long time', etc. — between the verb and the underlined phrase. What is the result?

1. He **sat** patiently <u>on the floor</u>.
2. * He **swept** patiently <u>the floor</u>.

Go through the rest of the examples and you will discover the same thing: you cannot normally insert other words between a **verb** and its **object**.

Does this mean that any time we see a noun phrase immediately following a verb (and cannot be separated from it), it must be the object?

QUESTION 6

In the following sentences, the verb (highlighted in bold) is followed by a noun phrase (underlined). Are all these noun phrases objects? If not, which ones are not, and can you explain why?

1. The typhoon **flooded** <u>many areas</u> and **destroyed** <u>many buildings</u>.
2. The typhoon **lasted** <u>one whole week</u>.
3. The night before the trip he **packed** <u>his suitcase</u>.
4. His suitcase **weighed** <u>thirty kilograms</u>.
5. He **hired** <u>an English teacher</u>.
6. She **became** <u>an English teacher</u>.

The following are not objects:

You'll probably have found that the underlined noun phrases in sentences 2, 4 and 6 are not objects. It isn't that easy to explain why they are not, and you may have your own way of explaining it. There is one grammatical 'test' that you can do, to find out whether the noun or noun phrase after a verb is an object.

QUESTION 7

Try turning the sentences in Question 6 into the **passive voice** — if you can. Sentence 1 is done for you:

1. <u>Many areas</u> **were flooded** and <u>many buildings</u> **were destroyed** by the typhoon.

2.

3.

4.

5.

6.

What did you find? Not all of these sentences can be 'passivized' (turned into the passive voice). And it is those sentences which do *not* have objects, i.e. sentences 2, 4, 6, that cannot be passivized.

And now, to summarize what we've found so far:

- There are two types of verbs: **transitive** and **intransitive**.
- A **transitive** verb *needs* an **object**, while an **intransitive** verb *cannot* take an **object**.
- An **object** is normally a **noun phrase** which immediately follows the **verb**, and which can be **passivized**.

Mistakes are sometimes made by students who confuse transitive with intransitive verbs.

QUESTION 8

Explain the mistakes in the following sentences, and correct them:

1. The figure raises.

Answer:

2. The financial crisis deteriorated the economy of Hong Kong.

Answer:

3. The employees want the boss to rise their salaries.

Answer:

Some Complications

Just as there are nouns which can be used both as mass nouns and count nouns, e.g. *cake, paper* (as in 'Paper was invented in China' vs. 'Many papers were presented at the conference'), so there are verbs which can be used both as **transitive** and **intransitive** verbs, usually with some differences in meaning. Take for example the verb *grow*. As an **intransitive** verb, it has several meanings, including 'to develop or increase over time', as in:

1. Papaya trees *grow* well in this soil.
2. The economy *is growing* at a fantastic rate.

As a **transitive** verb, it means 'to make plants grow', as in:

3. We tried to *grow* vegetables in our garden, but failed.

Let's look at some more verbs.

QUESTION 9

In the following sentences, you will find the underlined verbs used in two different ways — one transitive and one intransitive. Identify each of these uses, and explain any differences in meaning between the two uses.

1. He <u>flew</u> from Hong Kong to San Francisco, then drove to Yosemite.
2. He <u>flew</u> an old plane and nearly had a crash.
3. She <u>walked</u> to school yesterday as the weather was fine.
4. She <u>walks</u> her dog every morning before going to school.
5. He <u>drinks</u> tea but not coffee.
6. He <u>drinks</u> with his friends every weekend.
7. Tom <u>painted</u> the fence all by himself.
8. Do you know that Tom can <u>paint</u>?
9. You don't have to <u>run</u> every time your boss calls.
10. The boss <u>runs</u> his company like a military establishment.

1–2:

3–4:

5–6:

7–8:

9–10:

It is a good habit to look up a dictionary when you are in doubt about transitivity — transitive uses are identified by [T] and intransitive uses by [I]. In fact, it is a good habit to look up a lot of other things in a dictionary — how a word is used, what word class (noun, verb, adjective, etc.) it belongs to (words often belong to more than one class), whether a noun is countable or uncountable, etc. A dictionary tells you *much more* than just the meaning — it tells you a lot about the **grammar** of words.

The Passive Voice

We mentioned the **passive voice** earlier in this unit. As you know, we can change an **active** into a **passive** sentence by

(a) moving the **object** of the active sentence into the **subject** position in the passive sentence, and
(b) changing the main verb into the **past participle** form, preceded by the auxiliary *be*.

A third step is optional, and may be left out if you wish, and that is to take the original subject of the active sentence and moving it to a position after the verb, preceded by the preposition *by*. The following example illustrates both possibilities:

1. ACTIVE: The earthquake *destroyed* the whole village.
2. PASSIVE: The whole village *was destroyed*.
3. PASSIVE: The whole village *was destroyed* by the earthquake.

Whether you choose (2) or (3) depends on how much information you want to give, or how much you know about the 'doer' or 'agent' that did it. Sometimes it's not known who did it, e.g. 'My wallet was stolen'. Sometimes it is unnecessary or irrelevant, but sometimes it is extremely important. Let's think about these options by looking at the questions below.

 QUESTION 10

Give the passive forms of the following sentences. Decide whether or not to include information on the 'doer', but whichever way you decide, try to explain why.

1. Lee Harvey Oswald assassinated President Kennedy in 1963.

Answer:

2. Somebody invented paper in China thousands of years ago.

Answer:

3. We can divide all living things into two main types.

   Answer:

4. I.M. Pei designed the Bank of China building in Hong Kong.

   Answer:

5. Extraterrestrial aliens kidnapped my friend and took him up into their spaceship last night.

   Answer:

6. The police have finally arrested the kidnappers.

   Answer:

Turning sentences into the passive voice may seem like a mechanical procedure to some of you. The procedure itself may be simple, and yet students do make lots of mistakes.

 QUESTION 11

Given below are some mistakes made by students in the use of the passive voice. Correct these mistakes. At the end of this question, can you think of a reason why students keep on making such mistakes?

1. This vitamin can find in carrots.

   Answer:

2. It cannot produce by the body.

   Answer:

3. These results can classify three types.

   Answer:

4. Some giant plants were decay.

   Answer:

An Explanation

You may have arrived at your own explanation of why students make relatively frequent mistakes like the above with the passive voice. But here is another explanation that may interest you.

If you think about it, Chinese does not really have a 'passive voice'. This is shown by the following examples from Chinese:

1. *fan zhu hao le* (飯煮好了 = 'rice cook already')
2. *xin xie hao le* (信寫好了 = 'letter write already')
3. *shu mai wan le* (書賣完了 = 'book sell finish already')
4. *mai wan le* (賣完了 = 'sell finish already')

On the surface, these Chinese sentences look just like 'active' sentences, because the verbs are in exactly the same form. But there are two major differences between English and Chinese that you should notice by comparing the above sentences with their English equivalents:

1a. The rice is cooked.
2a. The letter has been written.
3a. The book is sold out.
4a. The book (or CD or magazine etc.) is sold out.

 QUESTION 12

Compare sentences 1–4 in Chinese, and 1a–4a in English, as given above. Describe at least two differences between the grammar of Chinese and English as revealed by these sentences (you may ignore differences in tense and aspect for the purposes of this question).

Comparing the Chinese and English sentences 1–4 and 1a–4a, we find the following differences:

(a) Chinese does not have a special verb form like the past participle (*written, sold*, etc.) which is associated with the passive voice in English. The form of the verb never changes in Chinese, whether in an 'active' or 'passive' sense.

(b) A Chinese sentence does not need a **subject** (as in sentence 4).

You may recall from Unit 1 that a Chinese sentence has a **topic** rather than a subject. In English, the passive construction is needed precisely because the **object** of the **active** sentence has become the **subject** of the **passive** sentence. But imagine a language, like Chinese, where subjects are not obligatory. All we would need then is a topic ('this is what I'm talking about'), and a comment ('this is what I'm going to say about it'). So in sentence 1 above, 'rice' is my topic, and what I want to say about it is that the cooking of it is done, or someone has cooked it — hence 'cook already'.

From this point of view, the idea of 'passive' would seem quite unnecessary in Chinese. We can now understand why the students wrote sentences 1–3 of Question 11 this way, e.g. 'This vitamin can find in carrots', etc. It's like saying, 'As for this vitamin, we can find it in carrots', but leaving out all the 'unnecessary' words!

The important thing is that English grammar does *not* work this way. Remember that:

- **The subject of the passive sentence corresponds to the object of the active sentence, and so the verb should take the passive (i.e. past participle) form.**

Passive Voice and Tense/Aspect

The passive voice can freely combine with the use of any tense, for example:

(1) Simple **present tense**: Nowadays, lectures *are held* in posh, air-conditioned theatres.
(2) Simple **past tense**: Decades ago, they *were held* in crude, makeshift buildings.

The passive voice can also be used in any other tense/aspect/modality combination, or even be non-finite, as in the following examples:

(3) **Present progressive**: Lectures *are being held* in the gym this week.
(4) **Present perfect**: Lectures *have been held* in the gym before.
(5) **Past progressive**: Lectures *were being held* on the podium while the renovations were going on.
(6) **Past perfect**: Lectures *had been held* in all kinds of places before the theatre was built.
(7) With **modal auxiliaries**: Lectures *will be held* in the gym if it rains. Or they *may be cancelled*.
(8) **Non-finite**: *Being called* a fool is bad enough, but being called a traitor is much worse. Do you want *to be called* both?

QUESTION 13

Fill in the blanks below with the appropriate forms of the verbs in brackets (please use them as **verbs** and don't change them into nouns or other things). Be careful with the tense or aspect or modal auxiliaries that may be needed.

1. After working for 10 years as a clerk, John hopes _____ (promote).
2. Students who are more than 15 minutes late for class _____ (treat) as absent.
3. When he arrived home, he noticed that all the lights _____ (switch on).
4. It is very humiliating to _____ (make) fun of by your classmates.
5. At the time the lawyer arrived at the police station, his client _____ (interrogate).
6. In my opinion, all computer hackers _____ (lock up).
7. These diseases _____ (spread) by physical contact, not through the air.
8. Do you know which films _____ (nominate) for next year's Academy Awards?
9. At the Asian Games, two of Hong Kong's table tennis players _____ (send) home.
10. We are not sure how he died. He _____ (poison), or he _____ (shoot).

Present and Past Participles as Adjectives

Recall that a verb has a **present participle** form (e.g. *breaking*) and **past participle** form (e.g. *broken*). You have seen that the present participle is used in the **progressive** aspect (e.g. 'He is breaking all the records'), and the past participle in the **perfect** aspect ('He has broken all the records') and the **passive** voice ('All the records have been broken').

There is another important use for these verb forms, and that is, as **adjectives**. For example:

1. The *breaking* glass made a loud noise.
2. The *broken* glass cut my feet.

In the above examples, *breaking* and *broken* function as adjectives telling us something about the noun 'glass'.

The important question to ask is: What is the connection between the **verb** in **present participle** (like *breaking*) or **past participle** form (like *broken*), and the **noun** that it modifies (like *glass*)? Perhaps you can figure this out for yourself from the following exercise.

 QUESTION 14

Analyse the sentences below, and state the relationship between the underlined verb (functioning here as an adjective) and the noun which follows. [Clue: Is the noun the 'logical' subject, object, or something else, of the verb?] What generalizations can you make after analysing all these examples?

1. The <u>hunting</u> party rested after a long day.
2. The <u>hunted</u> animals had no rest.
3. The <u>winning</u> team celebrated their victory.
4. The <u>defeated</u> team broke down in tears.
5. The <u>crying</u> baby kept me awake all night.
6. There's no use crying over <u>spilled</u> milk.
7. The <u>disappointing</u> Vanessa Mae concert left a bad impression.
8. Her <u>disappointed</u> fans demanded their money back.
9. The <u>exhausting</u> match lasted for five hours.
10. The <u>exhausted</u> players collapsed as soon as it ended.

Relationship between:
present participle (e.g. *hunting*) and the noun (e.g. *party*):

past participle (e.g. *hunted*) and the noun (e.g. *animals*):

If you have analysed the examples in Question 14 carefully, you will have found an interesting and systematic relationship between the present/past participle verb acting as adjective and the noun. The noun is usually the logical **subject** of the **present participle**. For example, in 'the *winning* team', the 'team' is the logical subject of the verb 'win' — the team won. In contrast, the noun is usually the logical **object** of the **past participle**. For example, in 'the defeated team', the 'team' is the logical object of the verb 'defeat' — somebody defeated the team, and the team was defeated.

 QUESTION 15

Some of the following sentences contain mistakes of the kind that we discussed above. Identify and correct these mistakes.

1. It was useful to study the remained parts of the plants.
2. A survey conducting among 100 chief executives has been published.
3. A million years ago, there were many giant plants grown on the Earth.
4. Their performance is really fascinated. I have seen it three times.
5. I was so boring with the math lesson that I went to sleep.
6. These confusing rules are impossible to understand.
7. The children seem delighting by the cartoon.
8. The little girl was frightening by the fierce barking dog.
9. The manager apologized to the annoyed customers.
10. The moving vehicle smashed into his rear.

Answer:

88   Understanding English Grammar

Now that you have a better understanding of transitivity and the passive, and the use of present and past participles as adjectives, let's do a few more exercises to make sure you've got it right.

Additional Exercises

Fill in the blanks with the appropriate forms of the verbs in brackets:

Text 1

The disruption of the Google search engine this month appears to have been only one symptom of a significant change in the way China censors the Internet. Observers say the main focus of the so-called Great Firewall has switched from preventing access to a long list of _____ (ban) Websites to screening Internet traffic, including e-mail, by searching out keywords and blocking the data they _____ (associate) with.

A far greater amount of online information _____ (deny) to mainland residents than was previously the case.

The changes, which began to _____ (notice) around September 13, are also proving highly unpopular with many of the country's 46 million Internet users.

News sites, including the *South China Morning Post*'s scmp.com, particularly _____ (affect). Mainland users can still reach the scmp.com homepage, but if they try to read stories on topics Beijing considers politically sensitive, they _____ (block). Even sites that offer seemingly benign information _____ (tamper) with.

After being off-line for two weeks this month, Google now works when users put in most words. But looking for information on a banned topic can cause searches to _____ (block) until the browser _____ (restart).

Text 2

Police are considering laying charges after a Chinese flag _____ (set) on fire during a National Day protest yesterday.

It would be the first time that a flag-burning prosecution _____ (bring) — although there have been five convictions for desecrating the national or SAR flags, the charge which could apply to the new case. In the previous cases, flags _____ (deface) or _____ (alter) by protesters.

Yesterday's flag-burning _____ (happen) when 10 members of the April 5th Action Group marched from the Southorn Centre in Wan Chai about 7 am. A dozen police officers _____ (escort) the group but stopped it near Central Plaza and asked to check what was inside the coffin. They _____ (demand) that the protesters move to a demonstration area set up by the police.

A minor scuffle broke out as the activists defied police demands and _____ (insist) on heading for the waterfront. During the confusion, a national flag _____ (set) alight. Officers _____ (use) a fire extinguisher to put out the blaze.

Ng Po-keung, the assistant Wan Chai division commander, said the protesters might have breached the National Flag Ordinance by burning the flag.

"We will investigate the incident of burning the national flag and seek legal advice from the Justice Department as to what follow-up action should _____ (take)," he said.

"Long Hair" Leung Kwok-hung, a core member of the April 5th Action Group, said he not _____ (involve) in burning the flag.

Leung, who is on trial over unlawful assembly charges, _____ (fine) $6,000 for desecrating the Hong Kong flag with his colleague Koo Sze-yiu during an anti-police rally in May last year.

Text 3

Legislators and tourism industry leaders last night demanded an inquiry after thousands of Hong Kong residents and tourists _____ (strand) at the Lowu border crossing because of a mainland computer breakdown.

Long queues formed on the mainland side when the crash happened at noon. It _____ (take) 45 minutes to fix the glitch, but some people said they _____ (delay) by up to two hours because of the knock-on effects.

It was an embarrassment for Shenzhen border authorities who, in response to complaints about border delays, _____ (claim) just five weeks ago that their efficiency was "even better" than that of their Hong Kong counterparts.

Many transit passengers were angry. "I have a plane to catch. What I _____ (suppose) to do?" shouted Cheung Wai-kuen, who said he _____ (trap) for 30 minutes and had less than an hour to reach Shenzhen's airport.

Tony Law Yau-tong, the border commander of the Immigration Department, said some travel agents should _____ (hold) responsible for the border congestion. He said only 173 mainland tour groups _____ (tell) Shenzhen border authorities of visits in advance but 250 groups turned up at Lowu yesterday.

"Most of the mainland tourists are only on a short trip to Hong Kong. It must be very frustrating if most of their time _____ (spend) on queueing up for border-crossing." Mr Li said.

Text 4

Canto-pop star Nicholas Tse Ting-fung will be spending two weeks in jail while awaiting sentence after _____ (convict) of perverting the course of justice on Wednesday afternoon.

    The Western Court ruled that the teen idol and 28-year-old police constable Lau Chi-wai were both guilty of allowing Tse's former chauffeur, Shing Kwok-ting, to stand in as the driver of Tse's black Ferrari when it crashed at Cotton Tree Drive on March 23.

    No sentence _____ (hand) down but Tse and Lau _____ (remand) in custody, without bail, until October 16.

    Last month Shing — who _____ (sentence) to four months' imprisonment after admitting to falsely representing himself as the driver — testified in court, under immunity for prosecution, that he _____ (ask) Tse to leave the scene of the accident.

    After saying he would deal with the matter, Shing asked Constable Lau if he could stand in as driver of the vehicle. Lau allegedly agreed to the request, the court _____ (tell).

6

Verb Complementation

Introduction

Learning the grammar of a language (to put it simply) is mainly learning about **what kinds of words or phrases go with what other kinds of words or phrases to form sentences.**

For example, what kinds of words would go with a **noun**? From what you have seen so far, they would include:

- Determiners (like *a, the, this, that, my, her*)
- Adjectives (like *good, bad, noisy, political*)
- Prepositional phrases (like *on the table, in Hong Kong, at the ceremony*)
- Relative clauses (like *who hates grammar, which I saw yesterday, smiling at me*)

We can 'build up' a noun phrase with one or more of the above parts attached to a noun, as in:

1. [The bad *student* who hates grammar] is going to regret it.
2. [The noisy *protesters* at the ceremony] were removed by the police.

Beneath the surface, there are actually quite a lot of similarities between the grammars of different languages, like English and Chinese. For example, in both English and Chinese, all the 'parts' mentioned above can go with a noun to form a noun phrase. Of course, there are some differences in word order — e.g. in Chinese the relative clause precedes (rather than follows) the noun head, as in:

1. 〔那討厭文法的壞<u>學生</u>〕考試不及格了 ([The hate grammar bad <u>student</u>] failed the exam)

92 Understanding English Grammar

What you'll need to do in learning English as a second language is to understand these differences and get them 'into your system'. This book helps you to focus on them better.

To refresh your memory a bit, in the last three units, we have been looking at what goes with **verbs**. First, there are **auxiliaries** that go with a verb to form a verb group, as in [*may have been* sleeping]. Then, we saw that certain verbs — i.e. **transitive verbs** — are followed by **objects**, as in [eat *durians*].

In this unit, we will look at verbs which need to be 'completed' by something else other than objects. A thing which completes something else is called a **'complement'**. Objects are the most common type of complement. Now we'll see what other types of complements there are. There exist a number of patterns in English, so let's explore them one by one.

Pattern One

Consider the following question.

 QUESTION 1

The following sentences are incomplete. How would you complete each of them? Try to keep it brief and simple. (NB: In case some of the verbs can be completed by an object, avoid using an object and try something different, just to see how it works.)

```
1. He decided _____.
2. He agreed _____.
3. He promised _____.
4. He wanted _____.
5. He intended _____.
6. He tried _____.
7. He pretended _____.
8. He attempted _____.
```

In trying to complete the above sentences after these verbs, you will probably have discovered two things:

Verb Complementation   93

(i) A *second* **verb** is normally needed to complete the first verb, for example:

1. He decided *to resign*.
2. He agreed *to repay* the money in full.

(ii) The second verb is in the **infinitive** form and normally begins with the 'infinitive marker' *to*. It would be wrong to leave out the marker, or to use a finite second verb, for example:

1. * He decided *resign*.
2. * He agreed to *repaid* the money in full.

 QUESTION 2

Think of *three* other verbs which are like the ones in Question 1, and make a sentence with each of these verbs:

1.

2.

3.

 QUESTION 3

The following sentences are taken from students' writings. Correct any errors that you may find.

1. Blackburn wanted Tom left DigiCom.

Answer:

2. Kevin wanted Angela marry him.

Answer:

94   Understanding English Grammar

3. Angela decided not see her.

Answer:

4. She told him don't look back.

Answer:

5. The heat made the mud becoming rock.

Answer:

The above exercise shows that some students are still unsure of the form of the second verb in completing the first verb. Let's study this a bit further.

Pattern Two

Look again at the first verbs in Question 1. There is another important point that we can make about them. Some of these verbs can take an **object** in addition to the complement, for example:

He wanted *his son* to be home before midnight.

But some others cannot take an object, for example:

* He decided *his son* to be home before midnight.

 QUESTION 4

Which of the verbs in Question 1 can take an object + a second verb as complement (like 'want')? Think of *three* other verbs which can also take an object + a verb complement, and make a sentence with each of these verbs.

1.

2.

3.

You will find a lot of verbs which take an object before the second verb. Besides the ones you have chosen above, just think of how many verbs there are like the following (the verbs are in bold and the objects are underlined):

1. He **persuaded** me to see the movie.
2. The captain **ordered** the soldiers to shoot.
3. The teacher **forced** the students to repeat the exercise.

What can we generalize about such verbs? It is quite obvious: these are verbs which normally require an **object** — i.e. they are transitive. Recall our discussion in Unit 5 about transitive vs. intransitive verbs. Take, for example, *persuade* or *force*. The act of persuading or forcing necessarily involves two participants: (i) the 'persuader' or 'forcer', and (ii) someone who is persuaded or forced. So these verbs require an object: 'The teacher persuaded/forced *the students* to take the test'. It would thus be ungrammatical to leave out the object:

4. * He persuaded to see the movie.
5. * The captain ordered to shoot.
6. * The teacher forced to repeat the exercise.

In contrast, take the verbs *decide* and *try*. They involve only one central participant, the 'decider' or 'trier'. So these verbs do not take objects: 'The teacher decided/tried to give the students a test'.

Pattern Three

So far, the patterns of verb complementation that we've been looking at, i.e. verb (+ object) + verb, all take an infinitive verb with *to*. That's the pattern in sentences 1–4 of Exercise 3 above. Sentence 5, however, shows that things may be a little more complicated than that. Let's find out more from the following question.

QUESTION 5

Are there any mistakes in the way the verbs in the sentences below are completed? If so, correct the mistakes.

1. I will allow him to go home early.
2. I will let him to go home early.
3. I saw him to pull the trigger.
4. I expected him to pull the trigger.
5. I heard him to say that you are his hero.
6. His father will make him to go to school.
7. No one can force him to go to school.

Answer:

You will have found that some of the above verbs (e.g. *let*) takes a second verb *without* the infinitive marker *to*. It is hard to make a simple, easy-to-understand generalization about which verbs require *to* and which do not. Meaning is not a reliable guide here. For example, sentences (1a) and (1b) below, and (2a) and (2b), are very similar in meaning, and yet (a) requires the infinitive marker *to* but (b) does not:

(1a) I allowed him *to go*.
(1b) I let him *go*.
(2a) I forced him *to go*.
(2b) I made him *go*.

Fortunately, the (b) type of verbs (those that don't take *to*) are much fewer in number, and so it is not difficult to remember them all (e.g. *let, make, hear, see, watch*). Notice that verbs that deal with perception (most commonly *see* and *hear*) normally take a verb without *to:* 'I saw/heard/watched him cry', etc.

To summarize what we've done so far, we have noted three patterns of verb complementation:

(a) **Verb + *to* Infinitive** (e.g. *I decided to go*)
(b) **Verb + Object + *to* Infinitive** (e.g. *I persuaded him to go*)
(c) **Verb + Object + Infinitive** (e.g. *I let him go*)

Generally, if the first verb is intransitive, it will take no object (as in [a]), and if it is transitive, it will take an object (b–c). One important thing to notice is that the object of the first verb also serves as the logical subject of the second verb. For example, in (1) below, 'me' is the object of the first verb 'persuaded', but it is also the logical subject of the second verb 'see' (i.e. I am the one to see the movie):

1. He **persuaded** *me* to see the movie.
2. The captain **ordered** *the soldiers* to shoot.
3. The teacher **forced** *the students* to repeat the exercise.

Likewise, 'the soldiers' is the object of 'ordered' but the subject of 'shoot', and 'the students' is the object of 'forced' and the subject of 'repeat'.

You may have noticed that a few verbs, like *want*, may or may not have a surface object, for example:

1. He wanted to become a doctor.
2. He wanted his son to become a doctor.

When there is no surface object (as in 1), what do you think is the 'understood' object? (1) can only be interpreted as: 'he wanted (himself) to become a doctor'. Thus, the subject of the sentence, 'he', is understood to be both the object of the first verb ('want') and the subject of the second verb ('become').

 QUESTION 6

All the verbs in the following sentences are capable of taking an object (underlined below). In which cases can the object be left out and be understood as the same as the subject of the sentence?

4. He persuaded me to see the movie.
5. The captain ordered the soldiers to shoot.
6. The teacher forced the students to repeat the exercise.
7. He likes his employees to be on time.
8. He convinced the enemy to surrender.
9. I prefer my children to have short hair.

Answer:

Pattern Four

Most verbs that are needed to 'complete' another verb (e.g. *escape* in 'He tried to escape'), will be in the infinitive form. However, with some verbs, this is not the only possible form.

 QUESTION 7

In the following sentences, the second verb is either in the **infinitive** or the '*-ing*' (**present participle**) form. Decide which forms are correct or acceptable.

1. He tried to break the window with his bare hands.
2. He tried breaking the window with his bare hands.
3. He wanted to give me a birthday present.
4. He wanted giving me a birthday present.
5. She prefers to play the guitar.
6. She prefers playing the guitar.
7. She convinced him to marry her.
8. She convinced him marrying her.
9. She heard him sing a Japanese song.
10. She heard him singing a Japanese song.

Answer:

So you've noticed that some verb complements can take either the infinitive or the present participle form. An interesting question is, do the two forms mean exactly the same thing?

Verb Complementation 99

 QUESTION 8

Given below are pairs of sentences, in which the verb complement (which is underlined for you) takes either the infinitive or the present participle form. Can you detect any differences in meaning? Think carefully, as some of the differences may be rather subtle.

1. I have seen him <u>cry</u> only once.
2. I saw him <u>crying</u> at the funeral.
3. He tried <u>to lock</u> the door.
4. He tried <u>locking</u> the door.
5. He stopped <u>to see</u> her.
6. He stopped <u>seeing</u> her.
7. The audience started <u>to applaud</u>.
8. The audience started <u>applauding</u>.

Infinite form:

Present participle form:

For an explanation of the differences, refer to the Notes and Answer Key section.

Pattern Five

Finally, there are some verbs which need to be completed not just by another verb, but by a whole **clause**. For example:

1. He said *that the future of Hong Kong was rosy*.
2. The headmaster announced *that the school would be closed on account of the typhoon*.
3. He asked his parents *whether he could have his own apartment*.
4. He does not know *how the money could have disappeared so quickly*.

QUESTION 9

Complete the following sentences:

1. The Chief Executive declared that _____.
2. He assured his parents that _____.
3. He doubted whether _____.
4. He wondered when _____.
5. The officer informed him that _____.

You will notice that the verbs which need to be completed by a clause, like *say, announce, know,* etc., generally have to do with communication or thought. The proposition which is communicated or thought of is naturally best expressed by means of a clause rather than a word or phrase.

Summing Up

The focus of this lesson is on verbs that need to be 'completed' by other verbs — in other words, on *verbs that occur in a 'series'*. In Chinese, you are familiar with verbs that occur in a series, for example:

他想去看電影 ('He *want go see* movie')
她決定不嫁他 ('She *decide not marry* him')
他上樓睡覺 ('He *go* upstairs *sleep*')

In Chinese, this is relatively easy — just 'string' the verbs together, as long as they make sense! There is no need to worry about the *form* of the verb, since verbs in Chinese don't change their forms anyway.

In English, however (as you have seen in previous units), a verb may assume different forms. The first verb in a series of verbs is finite, but the second verb is non-finite, and can take more than one possible form. In this unit, we have identified five main patterns. Some of these are more common than others. When you are in doubt about how to use a verb, be sure to consult a dictionary.

Additional Exercises

Fill in the blanks with the correct form of the verbs in brackets. There may be more than one correct answer.

Text 1

Before the invention of radio and television, people spent much of their leisure time (1) _____ (do) activities that required (2) _____ (do) or (3) _____ (make) something. They practised (4) _____ (play) a musical instrument or studied (5) _____ (sing).

Most people learned (6) _____ (keep busy) by (7) _____ (try) (8) _____ (improve) their abilities in some way or by (9) _____ (practise) a skill. People who couldn't afford (10) _____ (spend) much money on hobbies often started (11) _____ (collect) simple objects, such as matchbook covers or stamps, or even things like buttons or bottle caps. Of course, most people spent a lot of time (12) _____ (read), and (13) _____ (write) letters to friends.

Children played games in which they pretended (14) _____ (be) pirates or cowboys or people they remembered (15) _____ (read about) in books. Many women were extremely clever at (16) _____ (make) and (17) _____ (decorate) articles of clothing. Men often kept busy by (18) _____ (make) toys for children or (19) _____ (carve) small sculptures out of wood.

Text 2

Eliza Doolittle was a common flower girl who wanted (1) _____ (be) somebody. But she had a horrible accent, which prevented her (2) _____ (be) accepted by society. So she went to see Professor Higgins, a famous phonetician. She wanted him (3) _____ (teach) her to speak proper English, like a lady. He tried (4) _____ (get) rid of her at first, but when he saw how great a challenge it would be, he decided (5) _____ (take) her on as a pupil. He hoped (6) _____ (turn) her from a flower girl into a duchess, to win a bet with his friend Pickering. He promised (7) _____ (give) her free lessons. But he gave her a hard time. He forced her (8) _____ (say) the alphabet hundreds of times. He made her (9) _____ (speak) with pebbles in her mouth. He did not let her (10) _____ (eat) or (11) _____ (sleep) until she got it right. After a while she decided (12) _____ (quit), but he told her not (13) _____ (give up) so easily. In the end she helped him (14) _____ (win) his bet.

Text 3

The education secretary yesterday denied _____ (interfere) with the autonomy of two leading universities by _____ (voice) support for them to merge.

Secretary for Education and Manpower Arthur Li Kwok-cheung refused _____ (apologize) for _____ (say) on Friday that he would act as a "matchmaker" to speed the merger of the Chinese University and the University of Science and Technology (HKUST).

"What have I done wrong?" he asked. "What I had done was discuss _____ (raise) the standards of higher education with their vice-chancellors. It is up to universities now _____ (consult) the views of their staff and students on the merger. I will not be interfering with the autonomy of the institutions."

Chinese University vice-chancellor Ambrose King Yeo-chi, who supported the idea, said yesterday the two universities had yet _____ (reach) an agreement on the merger, adding no timetable for the move had been suggested.

Professor Li said he had discussed the merger with Professor King and HKUST president Paul Chu Ching-wu after joining the government in August. "We share the same view — that a merger between the two institutions could help _____ (develop) a world-class university."

He said he had expected his earlier remarks _____ (prompt) criticism. "Some people at the institutions may have conflict of interests and self-interests at heart," he said. Professor King supported amalgamation yesterday in a letter to staff and students at the Chinese University.

"A merger with the HKUST is likely _____ (speed) up the process for our university to develop as a world-class university," Professor King said.

But he insisted that the two institutions had not reached any agreement. "It should be decided after _____ (consult) staff and students," he said.

Text 4

The United States yesterday accused five Asian nations — China, Vietnam, North Korea, Laos and Myanmar — of severely _____ (repress) religious freedom as part of calculated bids to prop up totalitarian regimes.

The State Department named four other states in Asia — Pakistan, Turkmenistan, Sudan and Uzbekistan — as _____ (be) hostile to minority or non-approved religions.

The report's gallery of worst offenders targeted regimes which it said branded some or all religious groups as "enemies of the state" because of the threat they posed to dominant ideology.

China was accused of _____ (scrutinize) spiritual groups and in some cases of "harsh repression".

Vietnam was criticized for _____ (restrict) religious groups it deems in contravention of state policies. Some ethnic Hmong Protestants had been forced _____ (recant) their faith, the report said.

In North Korea the government continued _____ (suppress) groups not recognised by the state, the report said.

Myanmar was accused _____ (deploy) its "pervasive internal security apparatus" to infiltrate meetings of religious groups and the report cited credible reports that the armed forces had forcibly converted hundreds of Christian tribal Nagas to Buddhism.

The only non-Asian state in the same category was Cuba, where authorities were accused _____ (mount) surveillance operations against worshippers and of harassing unregistered religious groups.

7

Simple Sentences

Introduction

As you know, the chief aim of learning grammar is to be able to put words together to form **'grammatical' sentences**. (It is of course no less important to be able to write not only isolated sentences but whole **texts** — but for the purposes of this course, we'll start at the more basic level of sentences.)

So far, we've been looking at **parts** of sentences, such as the noun or noun phrase and the verb or verb group, because they have their own internal structures and it's important to understand them properly.

The noun (or noun phrase) and the verb (or verb group) can be said to be the basic 'building blocks' of the English sentence. Even the simplest sentence will have at least a **noun** —functioning as the **subject** — and a **verb**, for example:

1. People left.
2. The concert ended.

You can't have a complete sentence which is without either a subject or a verb — e.g. *'Left' or *'The concert'. [NB: For the time being, we'll exclude 'imperative' sentences like 'Go!', and sentences which are 'truncated' or cut short.]

A sentence is a very complicated thing to analyse, because it can be very, very long, consisting of an enormous number of clauses, for example: 'This is the dog that chased the cat that caught the rat that ate the cheese that Jim bought from the store that ... etc. etc.'

Or it can be very short, consisting of only one little clause (e.g. 'People left'). Though the number of possible sentences in English is infinite (we can sit here and continue making up sentences and more sentences until we die of old age!), it can be seen that they fall into a relatively small number of **patterns**. Understanding these patterns can help us to make grammatical sentences more easily, and this is what we are going to do in the next four units.

Since a sentence is made up of one or more **clauses**, let's first analyse the structure of the clause in English, and then the structure of the sentence will become clearer. A sentence which consists of only one clause is called a '**simple sentence**'. In this unit, we'll explore the structure of the clause (or simple sentence), i.e. the parts that it is made up of.

Pattern One: SV

(Note: **S** = Subject and **V** = Verb)

The simplest type of clause consists of a subject followed by a verb. Here are a few examples of this type of clause:

[Time]**S** [flies]**V**
[The war]**S** [has ended]**V**
[The new millennium]**S** [is beginning]**V**
[What he said]**S** [will be remembered]**V**

As we have said earlier, the subject is most commonly a noun (or noun phrase). But it is not the only possibility (as you may have noticed in the last sentence).

 QUESTION **1**

In each of the following sentences, can the underlined group of words function as the subject? From this evidence, can you explain what types of words or phrases — other than nouns — can serve as subjects? [NB: In case you don't know what to call the underlined groups in 7–9, they are 'subordinate clauses'.]

1. <u>Poor</u> are always with us.
2. <u>The poor</u> are always with us.
3. <u>Loudly</u> are here.
4. <u>The loudly</u> are here.
5. <u>Some</u> are here.
6. <u>On the table</u> is tiring.
7. <u>Standing on the table</u> is tiring.
8. <u>That oil floats on water</u> is well-known.
9. <u>What he does</u> is well-known.

> The following types of words or phrases can be Subjects:

Notice that, while a number of different forms can function as the subject (though nouns and noun phrases are by far the most common), only a **verb** can function as the verb. This may be obvious, but some students still wrongly produce sentences without a verb, e.g. *'Her father very rich', *'My friend very angry with me', etc.

Pattern Two: SVO

In Unit 5, you saw that certain verbs, called **transitive** verbs, require an **object**, without which the sentence would be incomplete. For example, *'He likes' and *'He hates' are incomplete, as opposed to 'He likes classical music' and 'He hates heavy metal'. 'Classical music' and 'heavy metal' are objects of the verbs 'like' and 'hate' respectively.

Here then is our second clause pattern: **SVO** (where **O** = Object).

QUESTION 2

Complete the following sentences with an object *only where necessary* (otherwise leave it blank).

1. My friend repaired _____.
2. My friend snored _____.
3. He caught _____.
4. He died _____.
5. The economy has deteriorated _____.
6. Workers' salaries will fall _____.
7. The building of Disneyland will stimulate _____.
8. The earthquake destroyed _____.

To test whether the 'object' you've added is really an object, try turning the sentence into the passive voice. Only true objects can be passivized.

Pattern Three: SVOO

In a SVO clause, there is only one object. But there are certain verbs that take not one but *two* objects. The most common example is the verb 'give'. In terms of meaning, the action of giving involves not only a 'giver', but also something which is given (the **'Direct' Object**), and someone who receives it (the **'Indirect' Object**). For example:

1. She gave *him* [**IO**] *an expensive present* [**DO**]
2. The university gave *the Chief Executive* [**IO**] *an honorary degree* [**DO**]

(where IO = Indirect Object, DO = Direct Object)

Notice that the indirect object *precedes* (comes before) the direct object — it would be wrong to reverse the order, as in *'She gave an expensive present him'. In this sense, English is just like Mandarin. However, there is another way of putting it, where the direct object comes first, and the indirect object comes next, preceded by a **preposition** (usually 'to'):

3. She gave an expensive present *to him*.
4. The university gave an honorary degree *to the Chief Executive*.

Again, this is like Mandarin — '她給一件貴重的禮物 (DO) 給他 (IO)', as opposed to the more common ' 她給他 (IO) 一件貴重的禮物 (DO)'.

Is it true that any sentence like (3–4) above can be rewritten as (1–2), with the indirect object preceding the direct object? This is a small but interesting question.

QUESTION 3

Some of the following sentences can be rewritten in the form Subject-Verb-Indirect Object-Direct Object, and some cannot. Identify and rewrite those that can. Do you see anything in common among them? [Clue: Look for any special characteristics of the indirect object in a S-V-IO-DO sentence.]

1. I sent a letter to my best friend.
2. I sent a letter to Japan.
3. She baked a cake for her boyfriend.
4. She baked a cake for the party.
5. He bought a car for his parents.
6. He bought a car for transportation.
7. He gave a thousand dollars to everyone.
8. He gave a thousand dollars to charity.

The sentences that can be rewritten as S-V-IO-DO are:

Pattern Four: SVC

(where **C** = Subject Complement)

We have seen that a sentence must have a subject and verb, and that some verbs need to be completed by an object. But are objects the only things that are needed to complete a sentence?

 QUESTION 4

Complete the following sentences with whatever words you find appropriate (nouns, adjectives, and so on, but *don't* use another verb here). If you use a noun to complete it, do you think it is the object of the verb? If not, why?

1. My neighbour is _____.
2. In the 1950s, Hong Kong was _____.
3. China will be _____.
4. He became _____.
5. These apples are _____.
6. The students seem _____.

> Types of words used to complete the above sentences:

You will notice that the sentences above are different from the SVO sentences that we looked at earlier. In the SVO pattern, the verb is 'completed' by an object, and an object has all the properties that we described in Unit 5 — i.e. it is usually a noun (or noun phrase), it can be passivized (i.e. moved to the subject position of a passive sentence), and in terms of meaning, it is the 'target' at which the action is directed.

In the pattern in Question 4 above, on the other hand, the verb is completed by something which is clearly not an object. It's usually called a '**Subject Complement**', and we'll see why in a moment.

A subject complement is different from an object firstly because it is not necessarily a noun (or noun phrase) — it may also be an adjective or prepositional phrase or subordinate clause, for example:

1. The economy became *very bad*. [adjective phrase]
2. The book is *on the table*. [prepositional phrase]
3. This is *what I've always wanted*. [subordinate clause]

Secondly, even if the subject complement is a noun, it can never be passivized like an object, for example:

4. He became *a stockbroker*.
4a. * A stockbroker was become by him.

Thirdly, unlike an object, a subject complement is *not* the 'target' of any action aimed at it by the subject. In fact, *it refers back to the subject itself*.

1. The economy became *very bad*. (the economy ← very bad)
2. The book is *on the table*. (the book ← on the table)
3. This is *what I've always wanted*. (this ← what I've always wanted)
4. He became *a stockbroker*. (he ← a stockbroker)

That's why verbs like *be, seem, become*, etc. are sometimes called '**linking verbs**' or '**copula verbs**', because they 'link' the subject to the subject complement. The term 'subject complement' suggests that it 'completes' the subject in some way.

Simple Sentences 111

One common mistake made by students is to omit a linking verb, especially the verb *be*, as in *'My friend ⌃ very angry'. This is partly due to the influence of Chinese, where the linking verb (*shi* 是) is usually omitted unless you want to emphasize the subject complement.

 QUESTION 5

Fill in the blanks in the following sentences with an appropriate verb. Some of them can only be filled by a **linking verb**, and some only by a transitive verb, so be careful. If a blank can be filled by either a linking or a transitive verb, then provide both, but note the differences in meaning.

1. He _____ a doctor.
2. The driver _____ a man.
3. My classmates _____ very hard-working.
4. During the trip, he _____ ill.
5. During the trip, he _____ a fever.
6. My teacher _____ a book.
7. My teacher _____ a singer.
8. The truth _____ that he had an affair with the intern.

Pattern Five: SVOC

In Section V, we saw that, in the SVC pattern, the 'subject complement' is needed to refer to and 'complete' the subject. As you can see, this is a very common pattern — there are lots of sentences like 'He *is* rich/young/handsome/ an actor/a teacher/at home/in the shower' etc.

There is a less common pattern where a complement is needed to refer to the object, for otherwise the sentence would be incomplete. That's why we call this type of complement an '**Object Complement**', to distinguish it from a 'Subject Complement'.

 QUESTION 6

There's something incomplete about some of the following sentences. Complete these sentences with an appropriate word or phrase. (For sentences which do not really *need* to be completed, do *not* fill in the blanks.) The objects are underlined for you.

1. The committee appointed him _____.
2. The committee welcomed him _____.
3. The students voted Professor Lee _____.
4. The students liked Professor Lee _____.
5. His war experience made him _____.
6. His war experience scared him _____.

The last pattern, SVOC, is the least common of all the five that we've seen so far, and involves a relatively small number of verbs (like *appoint, make, elect,* etc.) Still, it's important to know that such sentences would be incomplete and ungrammatical without an object complement where it's needed.

Adverbials

So far we have not said anything about a very common part of a clause or sentence. Consider the underlined parts in the following sentences:

1. He suddenly left Hong Kong yesterday.
2. He left Hong Kong for a conference in Tokyo.
3. He slept soundly on the plane all the way from Hong Kong to Toronto.
4. He cried because his sister took his teddy bear.

We'll call the underlined phrases **adverbials** — because they provide additional information such as the time, place, manner, reason, etc. (Note that the term 'adverbials' includes not only adverbs, but all other words or phrases [like the above] which have the same function as adverbs.)

The important point about adverbials is that they are generally *optional* rather than *compulsory*, and can be left out without making the sentence ungrammatical. All the other parts which we discussed earlier — subject, verb, object, complement — are compulsory (depending on the type of verb), and if any of them are left out, the sentence would be ungrammatical.

Another grammatical feature of adverbials is that, unlike subjects, objects and complements, they can be moved around much more easily. For example, sentence 1 can be rewritten as 'Yesterday he left Hong Kong suddenly' or 'He left Hong Kong suddenly yesterday', etc.

Simple Sentences   113

 **QUESTION 7**

Which of the bracketed parts in the following sentences are **adverbials**? Can you explain how you know?

1. He lent [her] [the book].
2. He bought [the book] [from the university bookshop].
3. The boss made [him] [the general manager].
4. The boss scolded [him] [all the time].
5. The light went out [all of a sudden].
6. The light blinded [the intruder].

The following are adverbials:

They are adverbials because:

As we've said, there is a huge variety of adverbials, and they are optional — i.e. not strictly required by the grammar. Therefore, we'll not say too much about them in this book.

Coordination

From the next unit onwards, we'll go beyond the single clause, simple sentence and look at more complex sentences. One of the most common errors made by students is to combine two or more main clauses (or simple sentences) into one sentence without any attempt to *connect* them. For example:

1. The economy deteriorated, many people lost their jobs.
2. I called yesterday, he was not home.

This may be due to the influence of Chinese writing. Just remember that in English, you cannot keep putting main clauses (or simple sentences) one after another in a series, separated only by commas. You will need to *join* them with **coordinating conjunctions**, like *and, or, but*.

1. The economy deteriorated, **and** many people lost their jobs.
2. I called yesterday **but** he was not home.

If you don't do that, you should at least separate the two main clauses into separate sentences, with a full stop:

1. The economy deteriorated. Many people lost their jobs.

 QUESTION 8

The following sentences are taken from students' writings. Correct any mistakes that you may find:

1. Vitamin A is also called retinol, occurs naturally in carrots.
2. The lower part was vegetation, this vegetation was very thick.
3. Coal is the most important fuel in our daily life, it has been used for a long time.
4. The baby was very clean, did not need a bath.
5. The giant plants died many years later, thus the plants decomposed gradually.

Answer:

Additional Exercises

Fill in the blanks in the following texts with appropriate words:

Text 1

I have read with amusement about _____ attempts of the Hong Kong government _____ control the littering public by _____ $600 on-the-spot fines.

As we have all seen by _____ reports about beach littering, this system _____ completely useless as it is.

I _____ like to propose a new three-phase scheme _____ would surely deter littering. Phase one _____ the same, an on-the-spot fine, but _____ to $1,000. Phase two would be _____ use the money to purchase a _____ refuse container to be placed on _____ near the spot of the crime. _____ this container would be a small _____ bearing the name of the offender _____ wording such as "This bin was _____ for by (offender's name) as a _____ of littering." Phase three of this _____ would be to make the offender _____ for one day cleaning the streets _____ the area where the offence took _____.

Surely this would deter littering in _____ of the punishment and I am _____ that it would also severely reduce _____ likelihood of a repeat offence.

Such _____ plan would demonstrate just how serious _____ government is about trying to make Hong Kong _____ a clean city, if indeed it _____ serious about a cleaner Hong Kong.

Text 2

The Chinese government will not let just anybody gather _____ 30,000 people, mostly students, in one place for an _____ or two for often emotional motivational speeches. Li Yang _____ clearly an exceptional case.

Mr Li is the inventor _____ Crazy English, a language learning method that requires students _____ shout in order to overcome their inhibitions, and he _____ more of a proselytizer than a teacher.

He once _____ to 100,000 people in a single day, at three _____ seminars in Chengdu, and to date as many as _____ million people are believed to have heard him speak _____ person or on tape. In perhaps the ultimate official _____, he was granted the privilege of holding a seminar _____ the hallowed grounds of the Forbidden City.

But it _____ not be surprising that government officials would support Mr Li, China's _____ English-learning guru. He is singing their song, and it _____ something like this: learn English because it is necessary _____ your life and your country, and in return you _____ be rewarded with a higher salary, a stronger China _____ eventually a future in which people around the world _____ be required to learn Putonghua just as they need _____ learn English today.

Text 3

I hope that I am not the _____ Hong Kong citizen to feel profound shame _____ the reaction, or rather lack of it, _____ our community to the bomb disaster _____ Bali.

The island is a popular tourist _____ for Hong Kong people, so it was _____ from the outset that some of the _____ would be SAR residents. Yet the only _____ from our city when the news was _____ was a rather bland announcement on the _____ of Cathay Pacific that it would send _____ larger plane than usual to accommodate residents _____ wanted to return early. While the Australians _____ sending in medical teams and supplies, we _____ not even bother to donate as much _____ a box of bandages.

Are we so _____ up in the never-ending debates on _____ economy and negative equity that we have _____ all sense of our moral and social _____? Even when it became apparent that a _____ of fellow residents were missing, no member _____ our accountable government was dispatched to the _____ to represent our community and to ensure _____ everything possible was being done to find _____.

The Hong Kong community seems to have sunk _____ a spiritual vacuum. We must examine the _____ for this and try to recover our _____ of humanity and compassion for others.

_____

8

Finite Subordinate Clauses

Introduction

There are two important things that you need to know about how to put sentences together grammatically in English:

(a) How to put a **clause** together (this was the point of Unit 7).
(b) How to *join* two or more clauses together to form longer and more complex sentences.

A **main clause** (or **independent clause**) is one which is capable of standing alone as a **sentence**, and if you can do (a) properly, then you can write simple sentences properly. (But be warned that 'simple sentences' may not be all that simple!) In Units 8 and 9, we'll focus on how to do (b).

At the end of Unit 7, we mentioned that we can join two (or more) main clauses together with a coordinating conjunction (*and, or, but*) to form a larger sentence, as in:

1. I opened the door *and* (I) let him in. [NB: The subject 'I' of the second clause is omitted because it is identical to the subject of the first clause.]
2. I warned him about drunk driving *but* he would not listen to me.

Such sentences are called **compound sentences**. Notice that each of the main clauses in a compound sentence is capable of standing on its own as a simple (but complete) sentence:

2a. I warned him about drunk driving.
2b. He would not listen to me.

If all English sentences were simple sentences (consisting of one clause only), or compound sentences (formed by joining two or more main clauses together with a conjunction), it

118   Understanding English Grammar

would be so much easier to learn how to construct sentences in English! But are the majority of English sentences in fact that simple?

 QUESTION 1

Analyse the sentences in the following text. Underline those sentences which are neither 'simple sentences' nor 'compound sentences'.

> The atrocity is above and beyond politics and partisanship. It would not have made any difference if the crime had been committed in reverse — if American terrorists had hijacked Afghan or Iraqi civilian planes and deliberately crashed them into the commercial centre of Kabul or Bagdad with the sole purpose of killing as many innocent civilians as possible. No matter what the cause may be, no matter which side of the conflict is right or wrong, nothing on earth could possibly justify or explain so heinous a crime against humanity. No civilized human being, of whatever persuasion (pro-American, anti-American, Christian, Muslim) would hesitate to condemn it in the strongest possible terms, and to demand that something be done against the perpetrators (whoever they may be). Those who could see something to cheer about at the sight of thousands of innocent people being blown to pieces or burning or leaping to their deaths had better look into their hearts, and ask themselves whether they are really human.

You will find that most of the sentences in the above text (and in most other texts) consist of more than one clause, and that most of these clauses are not main clauses but '**subordinate clauses**'.

Subordinate Clauses

What is a 'subordinate clause'? Let's think of a tree: it has a trunk, and several branches. If you cut away all the branches, you are still left with a tree, and it can still grow. But if you cut away the trunk, all the branches will fall and die, because they all *depend* on the tree trunk. Now look at a simple sentence, which consists of one single clause:

1. He was very naughty.

You can compare it to a 'trunk'. To this 'trunk' or 'main clause', you can attach other clauses, like 'branches':

2. <u>When he was a little boy</u>, he was very naughty.

3. He was very naughty <u>because his parents never taught him how to behave</u>.
4. He was very naughty <u>even though his teacher threatened to punish him</u>.

The underlined clauses above are like 'branches' which cannot stand on their own away from the 'trunk' or main clause:

5. * When he was a little boy.
6. * Because his parents never taught him how to behave.
7. * Even though his teacher threatened to punish him.

For this reason, we call these clauses '**subordinate**' (or '**dependent**') clauses. There is another reason: they tell you something more about the main clause, such as the time, place, reason, manner, circumstances, and so on. So, both in terms of grammar and meaning, subordinate clauses can be said to *depend* on the main clause.

In Unit 3, we have seen that the verb of a **main clause** *must* be **finite** (or **tensed**). A clause with a finite verb is a '**finite clause**'. For example, sentences 1–2 are finite, but not sentences 3–4 (which are ungrammatical):

1. John *bought* an apartment with his savings.
2. Mary *teaches* French in our school.
3. * John *buying* an apartment with his savings.
4. * Mary *to teach* French in our school.

So, main clauses must be finite. Do **subordinate clauses** have to be finite too?

QUESTION 2

Underline the subordinate clauses in the following sentences, and in each case say whether the subordinate clause is finite (F) or non-finite (NF) by circling the correct answer.

1. Because he was a tourist, he was easily cheated. (F/NF)
2. Being a tourist, he was easily cheated. (F/NF)
3. He booked his ticket early in order to be sure of a seat. (F/NF)
4. He booked his ticket early so that he could be sure of a seat. (F/NF)
5. Before he went to bed, he usually had a drink. (F/NF)
6. Before going to bed, he usually had a drink. (F/NF)
7. He told me that I should study harder. (F/NF)
8. He told me to study harder. (F/NF)

Thus, you've found that subordinate clauses may be either finite or non-finite. In the present unit, we will focus on **finite** subordinate clauses only, and leave non-finite subordinate clauses to Unit 9.

The Form of Finite Subordinate Clauses

A finite subordinate clause has all the 'parts' of the clause that we explored in Unit 7. Just as in the case of a main clause, we can find subordinate clauses with the patterns SV, SVO, SVOO, SVC and SVOC, with adverbials added if desired.

 QUESTION 3

Analyse the underlined subordinate clauses in the sentences below. Try to identify the various parts of the clause as S(ubject), V(erb), O(bject), C(omplement), and A(dverbial), by bracketing each part and writing the appropriate letter above it. In addition, in all these subordinate clauses, there is *one* word which does *not* belong to any of the five parts (S,V, O,C,A). Circle that word.

1. <u>Before the star arrived</u>, everybody was waiting impatiently.
2. <u>When the star finally arrived in a limousine</u>, everybody rushed forward to see her.
3. The singer had to cancel the concert <u>because he had lost his voice.</u>
4. <u>Since you are my student</u>, you'll have to obey me.
5. <u>After she had given him all her money</u>, she never heard from him again.
6. The committee told him <u>that they had elected him president.</u>

The Subordinator

Analysing the subordinate clauses in Question 3 will have helped you discover two things:

(a) finite subordinate clauses have the *same* basic patterns as main clauses; and
(b) there is one extra word which is not found in a main clause. That word is highlighted for you below:

1. **Before** the star arrived, everybody was waiting impatiently.
2. **When** the star finally arrived in a limousine, everybody rushed forward to see her.
3. The singer had to cancel the concert **because** he had lost his voice.
4. **Since** you are my student, you'll have to obey me.
5. **After** she had given him all her money, she never heard from him again.
6. The committee told him **that** they had elected him presiden.

This is an important little word, and it is known as a **subordinator**. As the name suggests, it introduces a subordinate clause. Without it, a finite subordinate clause would look just like a main clause, e.g. 'the star arrived' instead of '*before* the star arrived', 'they had elected him president' instead of '*that* they had elected him president', and so on. That is why the subordinator is so important.

Many students, however, make the mistake of leaving out the subordinator when it's needed. This happens particularly with subordinators like *that* and *whether*.

 **QUESTION 4**

In the following sentences (written by students), is there a subordinator missing? If so, fill it in. Correct any other mistakes that you may find.

1. A large majority thought oral skills were important.

2. There are different opinions about leadership ability is important or not.

3. The majority disagreed an attractive appearance is important.

4. The respondents considered appearance is not an important quality.

5. Scientists find the super carrot can inhibit cancer.

6. Do you know that how coal was formed?

This kind of mistake happens most often with the subordinator *that*. One possible explanation is that this subordinator — unlike *because, though, when,* etc. — does not convey any meaning of its own; also, there are no subordinators similar to *that* in Chinese (which has subordinators similar to *because, though,* etc.) And since 'that' can be omitted under some circumstances, especially after the verbs 'say' and 'think' ('I think you are right'), some students think they can omit it any time. If in doubt, it is safer not to leave it out.

QUESTION 5

There is a blank space in each of the sentences below. Fill it with a subordinator if you think one is needed.

---

1. He thinks _____ he is the cleverest student in class.
2. She said _____ she would come to my party.
3. Magellan proved _____ the earth is round by sailing round the globe.
4. Anne Frank wrote _____ she still believed human nature to be good.
5. He wanted to know _____ the flight had arrived or not.
6. She wondered _____ she would win the competition.
7. _____ the earth is round was known to only a few in ancient times.
8. _____ he is guilty or not has never been proved beyond doubt.
9. _____ I have not said a word does not mean that I have no opinions.

The above exercise will have helped you see the importance of the subordinator in introducing a finite subordinate clause in English — something that you don't find to the same extent in Chinese.

The Function of Subordinate Clauses

To understand the **form** of finite subordinate clauses is one thing. To understand their **function** is another, and in order to use subordinate clauses properly, you'll have to understand both. To put it simply:

- A **subordinate clause** functions as a *part* of another clause.

The parts of a clause (you may recall) are **S**(ubject), **V**(erb), **O**(bject), **C**(omplement), and **A**(dverbial). A subordinate clause may function as any of these parts (except Verb). Let's see how that works.

 **QUESTION 6**

The underlined subordinate clauses in the following sentences function as part of the main clause. What 'part' do they play in the main clause (S, O, C or A)?

1. <u>What I do in my spare time</u> is my own business.
2. <u>How the millennium bug would affect our lives</u> was not known until January 1.
3. <u>That a major earthquake will hit Los Angeles in the near future</u> is almost a certainty.
4. <u>Whether Mainland China and Taiwan can resolve their differences</u> remains to be seen.

Answer:

In the above sentences, the underlined subordinate clause functions as the _____ of the main clause.

In each of the following items, combine the two sentences into one by changing one of them into a subordinate clause. (You will probably find that this subordinate clause has the same function as the underlined clauses given above).

5. Hong Kong will be the site of a new Disneyland theme park. This has caused a lot of excitement.

Answer:

6. The continent of Atlantis may or may not have existed in ancient times. This has been debated for centuries.

Answer:

7. He gave up everything to become a monk. The reason puzzles me.

Answer:

8. He said something just before he died. It is known only to his wife.

Answer:

QUESTION 7

What part do the underlined subordinate clauses play within the main clauses of the following sentences?

1. He knew <u>that he was going to pass the exam with flying colours</u>.
2. He found <u>that nobody believed his story</u>.
3. She finally discovered <u>what her son was doing behind her back</u>.
4. Do you remember <u>how the trick was done</u>?
5. Tom gave Peter <u>what he wanted</u>.

Answer:
In the above sentences, the underlined subordinate clause functions as the _____ of the main clause.

In each of the following items, combine the two sentences into one by changing one of them into a subordinate clause. (You will probably find that this subordinate clause has the same function as the underlined clauses given above).

6. He found this out. His wife was having an affair with his boss.

Answer:

7. Matter is a form of energy. Einstein discovered this.

Answer:

8. He wrote something. I cannot read it.

Answer:

9. Did he pass the exam? He wants to know.

Answer:

QUESTION 8

What part do the underlined subordinate clauses play in the main clauses of the following sentences?

1. The news was <u>that the bombing was not an accident</u>.
2. The truth is <u>that nobody is perfect</u>.
3. The question is <u>whether the stock market is heading up or down</u>.
4. The mystery was <u>how he could have escaped under guard</u>.
5. Years of ill treatment has made him <u>what he is today</u>.

Answer:

In the above sentences, the underlined subordinate clause functions as the _____ of the main clause.

In each of the following items, combine the two sentences into one by changing one of them into a subordinate clause. (You will probably find that this subordinate clause has the same function as the underlined clauses given above).

6. No-one can succeed without self-reliance. This is the truth.

Answer:

7. Should we sacrifice principle to expediency? This is the real issue.

Answer:

8. This is the reason for his absence. He had to attend an emergency meeting in Beijing.

Answer:

9. Mainland China and Taiwan may come to a peaceful settlement. This is our hope.

Answer:

QUESTION 9

What part do the underlined subordinate clauses play in the main clauses of the following sentences?

1. I will contact you <u>when I visit Beijing next time</u>.
2. He lost his job <u>because he was too irresponsible</u>.
3. He suffered a heart attack <u>while he was playing tennis</u>.
4. <u>Although he was poor</u>, he gave money to charity.
5. Mozart could compose concertos <u>before he was ten</u>.
6. She disguised herself <u>so that her fans would not recognize her</u>.

Answer:

In the above sentences, the underlined subordinate clause functions as the _____ of the main clause.

In each of the following items, combine the two sentences into one by changing one of them into a subordinate clause. (You will probably find that this subordinate clause has the same function as the underlined clauses given above).

7. My flight was cancelled. The airport was flooded.

   Answer:

8. He saved every dollar he could. He wanted to put his son through college.

   Answer:

9. The building collapsed. He could not get out in time.

   Answer:

10. He lost everything in the earthquake. Still he is happy to be alive.

    Answer:

11. I saw a terrible accident. I was driving to work at that time.

    Answer:

You will find that the last function, i.e. as **adverbials**, is the most common function of subordinate clauses. Subordinate clauses often tell us something about the time, the place, the reason, the cause, the result, and other circumstances surrounding an event.

To sum up, here are the most important points that you should have learned from this unit:

- Subordinate clauses may be either finite or non-finite;
- **Finite** subordinate clauses have the same form as main clauses, except that they are preceded by a **subordinator**;

- Finite subordinate clauses function as *part* of another clause — as its subject, object, complement or adverbial.

Additional Exercises

Text 1

Fill in the blanks in the following text with a suitable **subordinator** (such as *when, where, because, while, after, as, if, that,* etc.), if you think that one is needed.

Three women died and 21 other people — 17 of them fire officers and ambulancemen — were injured yesterday _____ a fireball tore through a flat _____ a woman was apparently trying to commit suicide.

  The explosion, which rocked the 22-storey building in Tsui Chuk Garden, took place _____ firemen broke down the door of the flat in a rescue operation.

  In the evening, the charred body of another woman was found inside the kitchen of the flat _____ the blast occurred in block E.

  Four firemen were seriously injured with burns to their faces _____ another seven were in stable condition.

  Five other officers were treated and discharged _____ another was under observation in hospital. Four other residents in the block of flats were injured.

  Several of the rescue workers who were injured were in a lift on the way to the scene _____ the explosion sent it plunging from the fifth floor to the second.

Texts 2 and 3

In the following two texts, words have been left out at regular intervals. Fill in each of the blanks with a suitable word which fits both grammatically and in terms of meaning:

Text 2

China seems to be in the throes _____ a burgeoning English craze. More than 50,000 _____ attended this month's Beijing Foreign Languages Festival, _____ English was the star attraction.

  English programmes _____ being strengthened at all levels of schooling, _____ more university courses are being taught in _____ . With an eye on the Olympics, thousands _____ police officers, taxi drivers and public servants _____ being given English lessons.

Of course, it _____ not for the love of Uncle Sam _____ English syntax. Learning English is seen as _____ way for individuals to earn more money, _____ for the country to accelerate its rise _____ a world power.

"Li expressly espouses learning _____ in order to catch up with and _____ the West, a vision he shares with _____ government and many Chinese intellectuals," said Barry Sautman, _____ expert on Chinese nationalism at _____ Hong Kong University of Science and Technology.

Mr Li _____ that Americans expect Chinese people to learn _____ language, while they make little effort themselves _____ learn Putonghua — even while living in China _____. Chinese person's first response when meeting a _____ in China is usually to apologize for _____ English deficiencies they might have. Crazy English _____ targets this sense of insecurity with its _____ on overcoming shyness.

Text 3

After all, the proposals affect everyone and only fools _____ say that these proposals do not affect them. It _____, of course, true that 99 per cent of _____ Hong Kong population will never be traitors, or subvert _____ central government, or steal state secrets.

But do they _____ that the new proposals will have the effect of _____ the freedom of the press, the freedom of association, _____ assembly, of procession and of demonstration — all of which _____ vital to any modern and vibrant society such _____ Hong Kong? Do they know that if the freedom _____ the press goes, then no other freedom is safe? _____ they know that a community which does not enjoy _____ freedoms will produce people without creative or independent minds? Do _____ know that this lack of creativity and independent thinking _____ causing concern for the governments in Singapore and China?

_____, if you want your children and their children to _____ up without creativity, please support the proposals.

9

Non-finite Subordinate Clauses

Introduction

In Unit 8, we learned that **clauses** can be divided into two types: **main clauses** and **subordinate clauses**. Main clauses must be **finite** (i.e. have a finite verb, which is marked for **tense**). We also studied the forms and functions of some finite subordinate clauses.

It is important to know that, unlike main clauses, **subordinate clauses** can be either **finite** or **non-finite.** The following examples (taken from Unit 8) show both possibilities. The underlined subordinate clauses in sentences 1, 3, 5, 7 are finite, while those in sentences 2, 4, 6, 8 are non-finite (the non-finite verbs are given in bold print):

1. Because he was a tourist, he was easily cheated.
2. **Being** a tourist, he was easily cheated.
3. He booked his ticket early so that he could be sure of a seat.
4. He booked his ticket early in order **to be** sure of a seat.
5. Before he went to bed, he usually had a drink.
6. Before **going** to bed, he usually had a drink.
7. He told me that I should study harder.
8. He told me **to study** harder.

 QUESTION 1

Compare the finite and non-finite subordinate clauses in sentences 1–8 above carefully. Note down all the *general* differences that you can find between them. [HINT: There are at

132 Understanding English Grammar

least three general differences.] It is important that you try to work these out for yourself before reading on.

> The general differences between finite and non-finite subordinate clauses are:
>
> 1.
>
> 2.
>
> 3.

Non-finite Verbs

The first and most obvious difference you may have noticed between the two types of clauses is (of course) the following:

- The **verbs** of **finite** clauses are **finite** (i.e. have **tense**)
- The **verbs** of **non-finite** clauses are **non-finite** (i.e. have *no* tense)

We discussed tense in Unit 3. The verbs *was, could, went, should* in sentences 1, 3, 5, 7 above are finite and have tense. In these cases, they happen to be in the past tense, but they could very well have been in the present tense: *is, can, goes, shall*.

The verbs *being, to be, going, to study* in sentences 2, 4, 6, 8 are non-finite and have no tense. You will recall that there are three non-finite verb forms: **infinitive** ([*to*] *go*), **present participle** (*going*) and **past participle** (*gone*).

 QUESTION 2

The underlined clauses on p.133 are supposed to be non-finite subordinate clauses. Give the appropriate non-finite forms of the verbs given in brackets.

Non-finite Subordinate Clauses

Julius Caesar was a great Roman general who wanted to _____ (be) crowned emperor of Rome. _____ (fear) Caesar's ambition, Brutus discussed with his friends what to _____ (do). _____ (draw) together by their love of democracy, the conspirators killed Caesar in the Capitol.

Caesar's friend, Mark Antony, gave a speech at his funeral. _____ (speak) at the top of his voice, he asked the Romans to _____ (lend) him their ears. _____ (stir) up by his fiery speech, the crowd then turned on the conspirators. Completely _____ (take) by surprise, they fled, and a civil war followed. _____ (know) that the end was near, Brutus killed himself.

Subjectless Clauses

In Units 7 and 8, we've seen that a **finite** clause — whether it's a main (as in sentence 1 below) or subordinate clause (sentence 2) — must have a **subject**:

1. *Many innocent bystanders* were injured at the demonstration.
2. I heard that *many innocent bystanders* were injured at the demonstration.

If the subjects were missing, the result would be ungrammatical:

1. * ___ were injured at the demonstration.
2. * I heard that ___ were injured at the demonstration.

But what about **non-finite** clauses?

 ## QUESTION 3

Some of the underlined non-finite subordinate clauses below are ungrammatical. Mark them with a (X), and explain why they are ungrammatical.

1. <u>Driving to work this morning</u>, John saw an accident.
2. <u>He driving to work this morning</u>, John saw an accident.
3. <u>Disappointed with her performance</u>, the boss decided to sack her.
4. <u>He disappointed with her performance</u>, the boss decided to sack her.
5. Peter applied to ten different universities <u>in order to get into one</u>.
6. Peter applied to ten different universities <u>in order he to get into one</u>.
7. <u>To be eligible for a scholarship</u>, you have to be a permanent resident.
8. <u>You to be eligible for a scholarship</u>, you have to be a permanent resident.

134   Understanding English Grammar

> Answer:

From Question 3, you should have noticed the important generalization that:

- A non-finite clause does *not* normally have a subject.

The question you'll probably want to ask at this point is this: if a non-finite clause has no subject, then how do we know what it is about (e.g. 'who did what?')

QUESTION 4

Here are the *correct* non-finite clauses from Question 3. For each underlined non-finite clause, write down its 'logical' subject, i.e. what you understand the subject to be, even though it is 'hidden'. What common *pattern* do you see in all these cases?

1. (_____) driving to work this morning, John saw an accident.
3. (_____) disappointed with her performance, the boss decided to sack her.
5. Peter applied to ten different universities in order (_____) to get into one.
7. (_____) to be eligible for a scholarship, you have to be a permanent resident.

> Generalization:
>
> In each of the above sentences, the 'logical' subject of the non-finite subordinate clause is always _____

From Question 4, you should have discovered this general principle:

- The **'logical' subject** of a **non-finite subordinate clause** is normally the same as the **subject** of the **main clause** that it is attached to.

QUESTION 5

Based on the principle given above, what do you think is wrong with the following sentences? Rewrite them in a grammatical form:

1. <u>Swimming in the sea</u>, the salt water got into his eyes.

Answer:

2. <u>Destroyed by the earthquake</u>, the workers started rebuilding the houses.

Answer:

3. <u>Angered by the noisy demonstrators</u>, the speech was cancelled.

Answer:

4. <u>All the time talking on his mobile phone</u>, the operation was badly done by the surgeon.

Answer:

QUESTION: What's common to all these ungrammatical sentences?

Answer:

There are, however, some exceptions to the generalization that non-finite clauses do not have 'surface' subjects. We will avoid highly unusual sentences, and stick to the most common exception below.

QUESTION 6

Some of the following non-finite clauses are ungrammatical, but some are grammatical even with a surface subject. Can you figure out the conditions under which a non-finite clause can have a surface subject?

1. * <u>He to say such a thing</u> is terrible.
2. <u>For him to say such a thing</u> is terrible.
3. * It is easy <u>the monkey to climb the tree.</u>
4. It is easy <u>for the monkey to climb the tree.</u>

For a non-finite subordinate clause to have a subject, it must: _____

_____

_____

Subordinators

In Unit 8, we saw that a finite subordinate clause must have a **subordinator**, like *as* or *because:*

1. **As** <u>he has become a citizen</u>, he is entitled to apply for a passport.
2. He doesn't want to join the tour to Beijing **because** <u>he has been there before.</u>

Is this true of non-finite subordinate clauses too?

 QUESTION 7

The following sentences contain non-finite subordinate clauses (underlined), some with subordinators and some without. Which of them are ungrammatical? Can you explain why?

1. <u>As having become a citizen</u>, he is entitled to apply for a passport.
2. <u>Having become a citizen</u>, he is entitled to apply for a passport.
3. <u>Because having been there before</u>, he doesn't want to join the tour to Beijing.
4. <u>Having been there before</u>, he doesn't want to join the tour to Beijing.
5. <u>That being a Chinese</u>, he naturally loves Chinese food.
6. <u>Being a Chinese</u>, he naturally loves Chinese food.

> Some of the above sentences are ungrammatical because _____
> _____
> _____

From Question 7, you probably got the idea that a non-finite subordinate clause cannot have a subordinator. This is generally true, but it is not as simple as that.

 ## QUESTION 8

Both the finite and non-finite subordinate clauses underlined below have subordinators. Identify the non-finite clauses, and decide whether any of them is ungrammatical.

1. Since he became a Christian, he has given up gambling.
2. Since becoming a Christian, he has given up gambling.
3. When you ride a horse, be careful not frighten it.
4. When riding a horse, be careful not to frighten it.
5. Though he was defeated, he did not lose heart.
6. Though defeated, he did not lose heart.

> Answer:

You may have found that all the above sentences (1–6) are grammatical, including non-finite subordinate clauses with subordinators (*when, since, though,* etc.), contrary to what we found in Question 7.

Unfortunately, there is no simple way of generalizing about which non-finite subordinate clauses can take subordinators, and which cannot. The general idea is that a subordinator is *usually* not present in a non-finite subordinate clause, unless the meaning really requires it. For example, in sentence 2 above, if we leave out the subordinator *since*, it would be hard to guess at the exact relationship between 'becoming a Christian' and 'he has given up gambling':

2a. <u>Becoming a Christian</u>, he has given up gambling.

To indicate that the relationship is one of time (i.e. 'since the time he became a Christian'), we use the subordinator *since* to make this clear:

2. <u>Since becoming a Christian</u>, he has given up gambling.

Functions of Non-finite Subordinate Clauses

In Unit 8 we saw that finite subordinate clauses function as part of a 'larger' clause — i.e. as the subject, object, complement or adverbial of that clause. What about non-finite subordinate clauses? Do they have the same range of functions too?

 QUESTION 9

Each of the following sentences contains a non-finite subordinate clause, underlined for you. What is the function of each of these clauses within the sentence?

1. <u>Flying a plane</u> is an exciting experience.

The function of the underlined non-finite subordinate clause in this sentence is:

2. <u>Being chased by a vampire</u> can be very scary.

Answer:

3. He hates <u>being chased by vampires</u>.

Answer:

4. She enjoys <u>swimming in the sea</u>.

Answer:

Non-finite Subordinate Clauses   139

5. His favourite pastime is <u>to watch girls passing by</u>.

Answer:

6. His greatest regret is <u>not having studied harder in his youth</u>.

Answer:

7. <u>Attacked on all sides</u>, the soldiers had to surrender finally.

Answer:

8. <u>After finishing his homework</u>, he enjoys watching a movie.

Answer:

9. She opened the door and let the intruder in, <u>thinking that he was her husband</u>.

Answer:

10. <u>Having worked tirelessly for forty years</u>, he finally decided to retire.

Answer:

You will find that non-finite subordinate clauses, just like finite subordinate clauses, function as part of a larger clause — e.g. as its subject (as in sentences 1–2), object (3–4), complement (5–6) or adverbial (7–10).

QUESTION 10

Fill in the blank in each of the following sentences with a **non-finite subordinate clause**, using the appropriate form of the words in brackets, plus any other words that are needed to complete the clause:

1. _____ (escape, jail), he was arrested again by the police.
2. _____ (read, letter), he started to cry.
3. _____ (be, mother) is no easy task.
4. She enjoys _____ (watch, old movies).
5. His biggest achievement was _____ (climb, Mount Everest).
6. _____ (travel, Egypt), he saw the pyramids.

Summary

To sum up, in this unit, we've learned that:

(a) A subordinate clause (unlike a main clause) can be either finite or non-finite;
(b) A non-finite subordinate clause has a verb which is non-finite (not marked for tense);
(c) It usually has no surface subject, and its 'logical' or 'understood' subject is the same as the subject of the main clause;
(d) It is not introduced by a subordinator (unless the meaning requires it);
(e) Like a finite subordinate clause, a non-finite subordinate clause functions as part of another clause (as Subject, Object, Complement or Adverbial).

And now, to reinforce what you've learned, let's do some additional exercises.

Additional Exercise

In each of the following passages, some subordinate clauses (or parts of them) have been left out from some of the sentences. Complete the missing parts, making use of the words given in brackets — but note that you may also need to use other words of your own, such as subordinators (*that, when, because, if,* etc.), determiners *(the, her, this,* etc.), auxiliaries *(can, be, have,* etc.), and other words. Make sure that the parts completed by you make sense and are grammatically correct.

Text 1

_____ (read, report) about abode seeker Wong Lau-shi, I feel both sympathy and disgust — sympathetic towards the mentally disabled deaf and dumb girl and disgusted at the Hong Kong government.

Just what does it take to activate the government's discretionary powers on humanitarian or compassionate grounds? This 26-year-old woman has no one on the mainland _____ (take care), but has two able-bodied parents who can give her love and support right here in Hong Kong. _____ (send back, mainland) with no proper care available, she will almost certainly be taken advantage of in some way.

Text 2

A hidden army of obese Hong Kongers are living indoors for fear of _____ (laugh at), says an expert who released figures yesterday _____ (show) 29 per cent of the adult population is grossly overweight.

About one in 20 adults weighs double their ideal body weight and are classified as morbidly obese, Chinese University of Hong Kong dean of medicine Sydney Chung Sheung-chee said.

"That figure may come as some surprise because _____ (walk in the street) we don't see it," Professor Chung said.

"But the truth of the matter is _____ (morbidly obese, patients, stay, home); they don't want to be seen."

Text 3

_____ (Three Gorges Dam project, enter, next phase), critics charge that issues ranging from environmental protection to the forced relocation of 1.1 million people have yet _____ (properly, deal with).

"Despite two-thirds of the Three Gorges Dam construction project being finished, problems such as environmental protection and migration are not yet solved," said Kevin Li Yuk-shing, a researcher for the International Rivers Network, a US concern group.

The Three Gorges Dam was begun in 1992 and is expected _____ (complete, by 2009) at a cost of 198 billion yuan (HK$187 billion).

China hopes the project will control flooding of the Yangtze River and generate 84.7 billion kilowatt-hours of electricity annually, but critics have argued _____ (also, have, disastrous impact) on displaced people and the environment.

More than 1.1 million people living around the Three Gorges Dam area have been forced to leave their homes _____ (land, live on, flood) when the dam is completed.

There have been reports of resettlement funds _____ _____ (embezzle, misappropriate, illegally, use).

10

Relative Clauses

Introduction

In Units 8 and 9, we saw that a **subordinate clause** (both finite and non-finite) functions as *part* of another clause, by being its subject, object, complement or adverbial. For example, in sentence 1, the underlined subordinate clause ('what you said') is the object of the sentence:

1. I heard what you said.

'What you said' is an object just like any other object, e.g. 'a song' in:

2. I heard a song.

But there is one other type of clause which is even 'lower' than that. It is not even part of a clause (like a subject, object or complement), but only part of a **noun phrase**. The noun phrase itself may function as the subject, object or complement, but the clause is only part of that. Let's look at the following example:

3. I heard [a song which was composed by a 12th-century nun].

The clause 'which was composed by a 12th-century nun' is only *part* of the noun phrase [a song which was composed by a 12th-century nun], and the whole noun phrase functions as the object of the above sentence.

QUESTION 1

Underline the **object** in sentences 1–3, and the **subject** in sentences 4–6:

1. He knows the answer.
2. He knows that matter is a form of energy.
3. He knows the formula which Einstein discovered.
4. The rumour is true.
5. What he told me is true.
6. The rumour which he told me is true.

What you should have noticed in the above question is that the object in (3) is 'the formula which Einstein discovered' and the subject in (6) is 'the rumour which he told me', and that clauses like:

'which Einstein discovered'
'which he told me'

are only *part* of the noun phrases [the formula which Einstein discovered] and [the rumour which he told me] respectively.

Relative Clauses

The 'which he told me' type of clause is known as a **relative clause**. A relative clause is part of a **noun phrase**, and it 'modifies' (or says something about) the **noun**. Students make a lot of mistakes with relative clauses, or else avoid using them entirely, so it is worthwhile trying to understand and use them properly.

The first and most basic kind of mistake is to treat the noun and the relative clause as two separate things. Look at the following sentences:

7. The nice young *man* apologized to me.
8. The *man* who stepped on my foot apologized to me.

When asked what the subject is, many students would say 'the nice young man' in (7), but 'the man' in (8). In other words, they treat 'the nice young man' as one single noun phrase, but not 'the man who stepped on my foot', even though both 'nice young' and 'who stepped on my foot' modify (or describe) the noun 'man'.

Why should students make such a mistake? Part of the reason is that, in Chinese, everything that modifies a noun must come *before* it. Thus, sentence 8 in Chinese would be

8a. '〔那個踏我腳的<u>男子</u>〕向我道歉' ('[The step on my foot <u>man</u>] to me apologize').

Students would have no trouble identifying the subject of the Chinese sentence 8a as 'the step on my foot man' (那個踏我腳的男子). They expect the noun 'man' to come at the end of the noun phrase, and all its modifiers to come before it. But in English, they have some difficulty recognizing 'the man who stepped on my foot' as one single noun phrase, because 'who stepped on my foot' comes after 'man'. So here's the first point to remember:

- In a noun phrase in English, a **relative clause** *follows* the **noun**, but it still forms **one single noun phrase** with the noun (just as much as an adjective before it).

So all of the following are equally **noun phrases**, and all of them can be replaced by a single pronoun, 'he':

[the man]
[the nice young man]
[the man who stepped on my foot]
[the nice young man who stepped on my foot]

 ## QUESTION 2

In each of the following sentences, there is a **noun phrase** which contains a relative clause. Put brackets around each of these noun phrases:

> 1. The Egyptian plane which disappeared over the Atlantic Ocean was carrying nearly 200 passengers.
>
> 2. The news which most excited Hong Kongers in recent years was the Disneyland deal.
>
> 3. The teacher scolded the student who forgot to do his homework.
>
> 4. *Life Is Beautiful* is a movie which can make you both laugh and cry.
>
> 5. I can't stand people who smoke non-stop.
>
> 6. He finally got the job that he wanted.

146   Understanding English Grammar

 QUESTION 3

In each of the following sentences, fill in the blank after the underlined noun with a suitable relative clause:

---

1. The <u>bus</u> _____ is late today.

2. The <u>waiter</u> _____ was fired.

3. The <u>student</u> _____ was very happy.

4. She married the <u>man</u> _____ .

5. The World Trade Centre was the <u>building</u> _____ .

The Form of the Relative Clause

Relative clauses have a special form which makes it different from all other clauses. The first special feature is the most obvious, and yet it is also the one which causes the most errors.

 QUESTION 4

Here again are the sentences from Question 2, but this time with the **relative clauses** underlined. Circle the 'special' word which marks the whole clause as a relative clause:

---

1. The Egyptian plane <u>which disappeared over the Atlantic Ocean</u> was carrying nearly 200 passengers.

2. The news <u>which most excited Hong Kongers in recent years</u> was the Disneyland deal.

3. The teacher scolded the student <u>who forgot to do his homework</u>.

4. *Life Is Beautiful* is a movie <u>which can make you both laugh and cry</u>.

5. I can't stand people <u>who smoke non-stop</u>.

6. He finally got the job <u>that he wanted</u>.

You will probably have circled the words *which, who* and *that* in the above sentences. These words have a special name — **relative pronouns**. A 'pronoun', as you know, stands for a noun. So what do these 'relative pronouns' stand for?

 QUESTION 5

In each of the following sentences, the relative clause is underlined, and the relative pronoun is given in **bold**. What noun does it stand for in that sentence?

1. The movie **which** won the Best Picture Award was *Gladiator*.
2. The movie **which** I saw last week was *Gladiator*.
3. The actor **who** made me laugh so much was Roberto Benigni.
4. The actor **whom** everyone loved so much was Roberto Benigni.
5. The song **that** Celine Dion sang in *Titanic* was 'My heart will go on'.
6. The singer **that** sang 'My heart will go on' was Celine Dion.

> A relative pronoun always stands for the noun _____
>
> _____

It is relatively easy to decide which noun the relative pronoun stands for. It always stands for the noun *just before it*! What is more important is this: what **function** does the relative pronoun play in the relative clause itself? Lots of errors are made because of this. Is the relative pronoun the **subject** of the relative clause, or **object**, or what? Consider the following sentence:

7. The movie which made the most money was *Titanic*.

In the relative clause [which made the most money], where is the **subject**? There's a verb 'made', and just before it there is a relative pronoun 'which', but no other noun. Therefore the subject of this relative clause is 'which'. And 'which', as you know, stands for the noun before it, i.e. 'the movie'.

Now consider another sentence:

8. The movie which I love most is *Gone with the Wind*.

In the relative clause [which I love most], what is the subject? It is obviously 'I'. So 'which' cannot be the subject. But where's the **object** of the verb 'love'? ('love' is a transitive verb which requires an object.) The object can only be 'which', because there is no other noun within this clause which can be the object. And since 'which' stands for 'the movie', the relative clause means 'I love (the movie) most'.

 QUESTION **6**

Here again are the six sentences from Question 5. In each of the underlined relative clauses, what is the **function** of the relative pronoun — is it the subject or object of the clause? (Write 'S' or 'O' in the blank at the end of each sentence.)

1. The movie **which** won the Best Picture Award was *Gladiator*. _____
2. The movie **which** I saw last week was *Gladiator*. _____
3. The actor **who** made me laugh so much was Roberto Benigni. _____
4. The actor **whom** everyone loved so much was Roberto Benigni. _____
5. The song **that** Celine Dion sang in *Titanic* was 'My heart will go on'. _____
6. The singer **that** sang 'My heart will go on' was Celine Dion. _____

One common type of error made by students is to have an extra object in a relative clause in which the relative pronoun is already functioning as the object. For example:

7. * The movie **which** I saw **it** last week was *Gladiator*.
8. * The actor **whom** everyone loved **him** so much was Roberto Benigni.

There you have a double object — 'which' and 'it', 'whom' and 'him'. It's like saying * 'I saw *the movie it* last week' and * 'everyone loved *the actor him* so much'! So watch out for this kind of error.

The Relative Pronoun

Now we'll look a little more closely at the relative pronoun. The most common relative pronouns are 'who', 'which' and 'that'. 'Who' has another form 'whom' (used in formal English only) when the relative pronoun is an **object**, as in sentence 4 above. 'That' is an 'all purpose' relative pronoun which can replace 'who', 'whom' and 'which':

1. The man **who/that** created modern Singapore was Lee Kuan Yew.
2. The man **whom/that** everybody knows in Singapore is Lee Kuan Yew.
3. The city **which/that** attracts the most tourists is Hong Kong.
4. The city **which/that** people want to visit most is Hong Kong.

The **relative pronoun** 'that' should *not* be confused with the **subordinator** 'that', which introduces a subordinate clause rather than a relative clause. Compare the following:

5. I know the man *that* wrote this book. (relative pronoun, introducing relative clause)
6. I know *that* he wrote this book. (subordinator, introducing subordinate clause)

The differences between the two 'thats' are:

- The **relative pronoun** 'that' occurs immediately after a **noun**, but not the **subordinator** 'that';
- The **relative pronoun** 'that' functions as the subject or object of the relative clause (e.g. in sentence 5 it is the Subject), but the **subordinator** 'that' only introduces the subordinate clause, which has its own subject and object.

Now, the most common error that students make with relative clauses is to *leave out* the relative pronoun. Take a look at the following examples.

 QUESTION 7

Correct the errors in the following sentences written by students:

1. The early symptom of people lack vitamin A is night blindness.

Answer:

2. One of the plants contains carotene is the carrot.

Answer:

3. The heat came from the earth would make the mud become rock.

Answer:

In all of the above examples, a relative pronoun is missing. It is interesting to note that relative pronouns do not exist in Chinese, which is one reason why they are often left out by our students. In Chinese, the noun phrase 'people who lack vitamin A' would be 'the lack vitamin A people' (缺乏維他命A的人) — *without* a relative pronoun, and with the relative clause *before* rather than after the noun 'people'.

Actually, under some conditions, a relative pronoun *can* be omitted in English. But make sure you understand what these conditions are.

QUESTION 8

In some of the following sentences, the relative pronouns are left out. In some cases, the results are grammatical, but in others, they are not (*). Can you figure out the reason why?

1. The movie **which** won the Best Picture Award was *Gladiator*.
2. * The movie won the Best Picture Award was *Gladiator*.
3. The movie **which** I saw last week was *Gladiator*.
4. The movie I saw last week was *Gladiator*.
5. The actor **who** made me laugh so much was Roberto Benigni.
6. * The actor made me laugh so much was Roberto Benigni.
7. The actor **whom** everyone loved so much was Roberto Benigni.
8. The actor everyone loved so much was Roberto Benigni.

Answer:

 QUESTION 9

Answer the following questions, making use of relative clauses in your answers. Compare your answers with your classmate's.

Example: What kind of food do you like?
   I like food that is spicy.

1. What kind of person do you want to marry?

Answer:

2. What kind of person do you want the leader of your country to be?

Answer:

3. What kind of person would make an ideal teacher?

Answer:

4. What kind of television programs do you like to watch?

Answer:

5. What kind of place would you like to visit on vacation?

Answer:

6. What kind of apartment would you like to live in?

Answer:

7. What kind of books do you enjoy reading most?

Answer:

8. What kind of students get the highest grades?

Answer:

Non-finite Relative Clauses

Just as there are finite and non-finite subordinate clauses, there are **finite** and **non-finite** relative clauses too. Let's find out how we use them.

 QUESTION 10

The following pairs of sentences illustrate the form of finite relative clauses and non-finite relative clauses (they are both underlined for you). Based on these examples, can you describe their *general* differences?

1. Vehicles which are abandoned by their owners will be towed away.
2. Vehicles abandoned by their owners will be towed away.
3. Students who fail the test will be required to retake it.
4. Students failing the test will be required to retake it.
5. People who live on Lantau Island are very excited about Disneyland.
6. People living on Lantau Island are very excited about Disneyland.
7. Every suspect who is arrested by the police is entitled to legal aid.
8. Every suspect arrested by the police is entitled to legal aid.

The differences are:
(1) Finite relative clauses _____
(2) Non-finite relative clauses: _____

 QUESTION 11

Fill in the blanks below with **non-finite** relative clauses, making use of the words given in brackets and taking special care with the form of the verb.

1. Students _____ (plan to study abroad) must apply for a student visa.
2. Towns _____ (destroy, earthquake) will be rebuilt with international aid.

3. Motorists _____ (drive trough the burning tunnel) were overcome by the heavy smoke.

4. The most important drug _____ (discover in the 20th century) was penicillin.

Existential Constructions

There is one common grammatical construction in English which often makes use of relative clauses, and which is the cause of some errors. First, let's see what it is.

 QUESTION 12

Read the following text, about the great detective Sherlock Holmes. Pay particular attention to the underlined expressions, and how they are used.

> Sherlock Holmes, the famous detective, was once taken to a house where a murder had apparently taken place. This was how his partner Dr Watson described the scene:
>
> When we arrived at the house, <u>there were</u> dozens of people <u>standing</u> around and <u>pointing</u> at the upper floor. We went upstairs into a large, empty room. <u>There were</u> no windows <u>which were</u> open. <u>There was</u> a dead body <u>lying</u> in the middle of the room. It was that of a stout, middle-age man. <u>There were</u> no visible wounds on him, but <u>there was</u> a pool of blood a few feet away. <u>There were</u> no signs of a struggle. The floor was dusty, and <u>there were</u> clear footprints <u>going</u> round and round the body. On the wall, <u>there was</u> a word <u>written</u> in blood: 'Rache'.

Now, without looking at the text, try to describe whatever details you can remember.

You will notice that, in the above text, there are a lot of sentences or clauses which begin with the expression 'there be (is/are/was/were) ...' Why do you think this construction is called the 'existential' construction'? Because it is a way of pointing to the existence of something not mentioned earlier. To better understand the function of this construction, compare the (a) sentences with the (b) sentences in the following question.

 **QUESTION 13**

Which sounds better to you, the (a) or (b) sentences? Do you have any idea why?

1a. A man is looking for you.
1b. There is a man looking for you.
2a. A book is on the table.
2b. There is a book on the table.
3a. A word was written on the wall.
3b. There was a word written on the wall.
4a. A country has 10 times as many sheep as people.
4b. There is a country which has 10 times as many sheep as people.

Answer:

Now try giving the Chinese equivalents of the above English sentences. (The Chinese equivalent for 'there is/are ...' is ' 有 ...'.) Which ones sound better in Chinese, the (a) or (b) sentences?

Answer:

You may have come up with a very good explanation why the sentences with 'there is/are' above (or ' 有 ' in Chinese) sound better. Now compare it with the following explanation.

You will recall that a **noun** can be used in a **definite** or **indefinite** sense. If it's indefinite, it refers to someone or something which is mentioned *for the first time* in this exchange, e.g.

(1a) *A man* is looking for you.

In English this sounds a little odd (not wrong, just a little odd), and in Chinese it sounds much worse. The meaning itself is perfectly clear — that's not the problem. But it's unusual to begin a sentence with something coming out of nowhere, which is what we get when we have an **indefinite subject** (like 'a man'). It doesn't 'connect' with anything we've said before, or anything already in the minds of the speaker and hearer.

Now, starting the sentence with 'there is ...', or ' 有 ...' in Chinese, prepares us by drawing our attention to the existence of something not mentioned before:

(1b) *There is* a man looking for you.
有一個人在找你

The similarities between English and Chinese in this respect may make it easier for you to learn the existential construction 'there is/are'. But there are three important points that you must be careful about.

Point (1): The existential construction '有 ...' is used much more often in Chinese than the existential construction 'there is/are ...' in English. So don't overuse it in English.

Point (2): Some students treat the Chinese '有' as equivalent to the English 'have', and produce ungrammatical sentences like the following (some are not even existential sentences):

1. * Normally, it *had* about 30 metres high.
2. * It includes some giant plants that *have* 30 meter high.
3. * There *had* some environmental changes.

In English, 'have' *cannot* be used this way. The existential verb, i.e. the verb which indicates the existence of something, is *not* 'have' but 'be'. The 'have/had' in the above sentences should be replaced by 'was/are/were':

1. Normally, it *was* about 30 metres high.
2. It includes some giant plants that *are* 30 meter high.
3. There *were* some environmental changes.

Point (3): The form of the existential construction in English differs from Chinese in one important way. Let's see if you can identify it.

 ## QUESTION 14

The following sentences were written by students. Correct any mistakes that you may find.

1. There were over 80% of them agreed with that.

Answer:

2. There were about 23 percent of them disagreed with the importance of leadership ability.

Answer:

3. There are many students study in the library.

   Answer:

4. There was a large number of people worked in the wholesale industry.

   Answer:

We want to draw your attention to one interesting thing. The sentences in (1–4) above are all ungrammatical. But try removing the expression 'there is/are/were', and what have we got?

5. Over 80% of them agreed with that.
6. About 23 percent of them disagreed with the importance of leadership ability.
7. Many students study in the library.
8. A large number of people worked in the wholesale industry.

Notice that all these sentences are now grammatical! What does this mean? This means that the students who wrote sentences 1–4 have taken 'normal' sentences like 5–8, and merely *added* the expression 'there is/are/were' to the beginning. They thought it would be a perfectly correct thing to do — but it is not!

But in Chinese, they would be right: this is how you would do it in Chinese — simply add '有' to the beginning of a normal sentence, and the result would be equally grammatical. You don't have to change a thing in the original sentence.

But English does *not* work this way. The sentences marked with * below, which would be fine in Chinese, are ungrammatical in English:

1a. A man is washing the car.
1b. * *There is* a man is washing the car.
2a. A man has been arrested 20 times by the police.
2b. * *There is* a man has been arrested 20 times by the police.
3a. A student scored 8 distinctions in the exam.
3b. * *There was* a student scored 8 distinctions in the exam.

So make sure that you get this important point about existential constructions:
- In English (unlike Chinese), you *cannot* just add 'there is/are' to the beginning of a regular sentence and leave the rest unchanged.

What then do we have to do to produce a grammatical sentence with 'there is/are ...'?

Relative Clauses 157

 QUESTION 15

Study the examples below, which are all grammatical. By comparing the pairs of sentences ('a' and 'b'), try to describe what changes have to be made to the original main clause (a) in order to turn it into an **existential** sentence (b):

1a. A man *is washing* the car.
1b. *There is* a man *washing* the car.
2a. A man *has been arrested* 20 times by the police.
2b. *There is* a man *who has been arrested* 20 times by the police.
3a. A student *scored* 8 distinctions in the exam.
3b. *There was* a student *who scored* 8 distinctions in the exam.

To change sentence (a) into an existential sentence (b), you'll have to: _____

_____, OR

_____.

This is what you should have found:

If the existential marker 'there is/are' is attached to a main clause, then we'll have to change it into either:

- a **finite relative clause** — as in (2b): There is a man *who has been arrested 20 times by the police*. Or:
- a **non-finite relative clause** — as in (1b): There is a man *washing the car* (where the verb 'washing' is non-finite and the relative pronoun 'who' is left out).

This is the big difference between English and Chinese existential constructions. In English, the clause that follows 'there is/are ...' cannot be a main clause, but a relative clause, because the main clause is now 'there is/are ...'

 QUESTION 16

Fill in the blanks in the sentences on p.158, using the correct form of the verb in brackets, plus any other words needed:

1. There are 5 books _____ (recommend) by the teacher as essential.
2. There were many people _____ (sleep) on the floor after the party.
3. There was a student _____ (say) that the subject was boring.
4. There will be many students _____ (apply) for the new course.
5. Is there anyone _____ (wait) for the bus?

Afterword

We have now reached the end of this book — but not (of course) the end of our study of grammar. No matter what your aim is when beginning a course on grammar, you always end with the realization that you have only begun to scratch the surface. Such is the richness and variety of language.

It has not been the purpose of this book to try to cover as much of English grammar as possible within its modest 200 or so pages. Rather, we have tried to help you to think about the basic structures of English grammar, and to discover important grammatical regularities for yourself, in a way that makes sense.

If you are interested in reading further on English grammar, a small number of books are recommended in the Bibliography at the end of the book; all of them cover English grammar much more fully than this book, and will certainly extend your knowledge of English grammar considerably.

But remember that, even more valuable than reading about grammar is the ability to notice, analyse and understand grammatical features in the language that you come into contact with every day, in newspapers, books, broadcasts, and so on. This is what 'lifelong learning' and 'independent learning' means, a process which never ends, and which is much more valuable than the finite knowledge that you gain from reading any books on grammar. If this book has succeeded (in some small way) in helping you develop the habit of noticing and analysing grammatical structures and relating them to your own use of language, it will have accomplished its purpose.

No-one is a better judge of a textbook than those who actually use it. The author welcomes your feedback, and can be reached at: tonyhung@hkbu.edu.hk.

Notes and Answer Key

In this section, you will find answers to the questions in the main text, which will enable you to check your own answers without the help of a teacher. Please do *not* look at these answers until you have attempted to do the questions yourself!

Here you will also find further explanations of some of the more complicated points of grammar introduced in the main text.

Introduction

The purpose of the Introduction is to make you more aware of an important point, i.e., every language has its own ways of putting words together to form sentences — this is what we call **grammar**. To know English is not just to know English words, but to know *how to put the words together* to form grammatically correct sentences.

It is important that you think about the regular *patterns* in which words are put together. Once you have acquired a grammatical pattern (such as 'subject + verb + object'), it is extremely powerful, because it will enable you to produce an *infinite* number of sentences of the same pattern in English.

The good news is that the number of possible grammatical patterns in any language (including English) is rather limited. So it's well worth your effort, and within your power, to acquire them.

The 'bad' news is that it is no use *just* learning the 'rules'. The so-called 'rules' of grammar are merely statements about the grammatical patterns of a language. 'Knowing' them is not the same as *acquiring* the ability to produce grammatical sentences. I can tell you the rules and you may remember them for a day and then forget them. To really acquire the grammar of English, it would be much more helpful for you to start with the data — i.e. grammatical as well as ungrammatical sentences — and work out *for yourself* the grammatical patterns behind these sentences. In this way, you can build up *your own* 'internal' system of grammar, which is likely to stay with you much longer than any list of rules that are handed down to you by the teacher.

To benefit from this course, you must take the time and effort to work out the answers to the questions, even if some of them may appear to be quite simple. As in mathematics, there is no value in finding out the answers from someone else — you'll learn nothing that way. The learning is in the effort that you put in to work out the answers for yourself. The teacher's role is to guide you through the more difficult problems, and to make sure that the patterns that you have generalized from the data are on the right track.

Suggested answers

(NB: These brief answers are only meant as a check on whether you're on the right track, and are *not* meant to be 'learned'. The real learning is in trying to find your own answers to the problems.)

QUESTION 1

Nos. 1 and 2.

QUESTION 2

There's something wrong with the word order: the adverbial 'yesterday' is in the wrong place.

QUESTION 3

For Chinese, the results are (* = ungrammatical):

1. √ Yesterday she met her friend. (昨天她碰到了她朋友。)
2. √ She yesterday met her friend. (她昨天碰到了她朋友。)
3. * She met yesterday her friend. (她碰到了昨天她朋友。)
4. * She met her friend yesterday. (她碰到了她朋友昨天。)

In English but not Chinese, an adverbial like 'yesterday' can occur at the end of the sentence; in Chinese but not English, 'yesterday' can occur between the subject and the verb.

QUESTION 4

There may be more than one possible answer (for both the grammatical and ungrammatical sentences), but the following seem to be the most 'natural':

a. Grammatical Sentences

English	Chinese
1. Our teacher left the classroom suddenly.	'Our teacher suddenly left the classroom.' (我們的老師突然離開了教室。)
2. I bought a house last year.	'I last year bought a house.' (我去年買了一所房子。)
3. He opened the window with a screwdriver.	'He with a screwdriver opened the window.' (他用螺絲刀打開了窗戶。)

b. Ungrammatical Sentences

English	Chinese
1. * Our teacher left suddenly the classroom.	* 'Our teacher left the classroom suddenly.' (我們的老師離開了教室突然。)
2. * I last year bought a house.	* 'I bought a house last year.' (我買了一所房子去年。)
3. * He with a screwdriver opened the window.	* 'He opened the window with a screwdriver.' (他打開了窗戶用螺絲刀。)

QUESTION 5

In both English and Chinese, the subject regularly precedes the verb, and the verb regularly precedes the object. In English but not Chinese, an **adverbial** (about time, manner, place, etc.) can occur at the end of a sentence; in Chinese, it must occur before the verb.

Unit 1: The Subject

The Subject is one of those features of English grammar which have proved both easy and difficult for Chinese learners — easy because there seems to be something similar to the concept of 'subject' in Chinese, and difficult because the 'subject' does not work in quite the same way in Chinese as in English, and most of the mistakes made by Chinese learners of English with respect to the subject may be traced to these differences. So it would be worth your while to pay particular attention to it.

In Unit 1 we discussed the main features of subject-verb agreement. To avoid making the overall picture too complicated, we've left out special cases of subject-verb agreement and put them in this section. You may want to read about them at your leisure.

Some special cases

Subjects that follow verbs

Though the subject normally precedes the verb, there are cases where they follow the verb instead (especially if the sentence begins with 'there is/are'). Even in these cases, the verb still has to agree with the subject, e.g.:

> On the floor **was** a dead **body**.
> On the floor **were** several dead **bodies**.
> There **is** a doctor on the plane.
> There **are** surprisingly few **people** at the concert.

 QUESTION 13

Fill in the blanks with a verb in the correct form, paying special attention to subject-verb agreement:

1. There _____ many people who would just keep quiet about it.
2. There _____ a quality which is universally admired in all cultures.
3. In the middle of the square _____ a statue of the great leader.
4. On the shelf _____ many books on music.

Collective nouns

A **collective noun** refers to a group of people or things which forms some sort of unit, for example:

army	audience	class	committee	couple
crew	family	flock	government	herd
navy	orchestra	public	staff	team

When a collective noun is used to refer to the group as a whole, it normally takes a singular verb, e.g.:

> The **audience** <u>is</u> waiting.
> The **team** <u>was</u> badly beaten.
> The **class** <u>seems</u> very quiet this morning.

However, when a collective noun refers to the group as a number of individuals, a plural verb is normally preferred. For example:

> The **audience** <u>are</u> stamping their feet.
> [NB: Would you find 'The audience is stamping its feet' somewhat strange? Why?]

*The **team** <u>were</u> very upset by their defeat.*
*The **class** never discuss their personal problems with the teacher.*

QUESTION 14

In the following sentences, a collective noun is used twice. In one case, it is more appropriate to treat it as singular, and in the other case, as plural. Decide which is more appropriate in each case, and fill in the blanks with the correct form of the verb provided:

1. The committee _____ (have) unanimously passed the motion.
2. The committee _____ (be) very upset by the bad publicity.
3. His family _____ (have) not spoken to him for years.
4. His family _____ (be) the most important thing in his life.
5. The public _____ (be) showing strong support for the new president.
6. Though the public _____ (have) different opinions on the issue, efforts are still being made to reach a consensus.

Adjectives as subjects

A small number of adjectives (preceded by the definite article) — especially those describing people, such as *the young, the rich,* and *the homeless* — can serve as subjects, and they always take plural verbs.

__The young want__ to grow up fast and __the old wish__ to grow younger.
Is it true that __the rich are__ getting richer and __the poor are__ getting poorer?

Suggested answers

QUESTION 1

The subjects are:
1. *Singapore* is the smallest republic in the world.
2. *The smallest republic in the world* is Singapore.

QUESTION 2

One possible answer: The subject occurs at the beginning of the sentence.

QUESTION 3

The subject immediately precedes the verb.

QUESTION 4

The subject controls the form of the verb [or: The verb agrees in form with the subject] in 'number' (singular/plural).

QUESTION 5

The subject and the auxiliary verb change positions in a question.

QUESTION 6

<u>Dictionaries</u> are full of words, and <u>words</u> are common property. <u>This sentence</u> itself is made up of words <u>which</u> can all be found in any English dictionary — and yet <u>the sentence</u> is not common property. <u>This</u> is because <u>words</u> are not used in isolation, but are put together by the writer, and <u>the resulting phrases and sentences</u> are products of his mind. <u>An idea</u> may be quite commonplace: for example, <u>the first sentence in this paragraph</u> contains a perfectly common idea, which <u>most of you</u> will have thought of at one time or another. Yet <u>the way the idea</u> is expressed is entirely my own, and <u>it</u> is possible that <u>no-one else</u> has written exactly the same sentence before.

QUESTION 7

(Here are the subjects originally used by the writer of this text. Other answers may also be acceptable.)

What is science? <u>The word</u> is usually used to mean one of three things, or a mixture of them. <u>I</u> do not think <u>we</u> need to be precise – <u>it</u> is not always a good idea to be too precise. <u>Science</u> means, sometimes, a special method of finding things out. Sometimes <u>it</u> means the body of knowledge arising from the things found out. <u>It</u> may also mean the new things <u>you</u> (or <u>we</u>) can do when <u>you</u> (or <u>we</u>) have found something out, or the actual doing of new things.

QUESTION 8

There's a separate topic and subject in some of the sentences, and they both refer to the same thing. Therefore one of them is redundant. The following answers are better:

1. Graph 1 shows that the standard of living in Hong Kong is rising.
2. The findings reveal that red wine is good for your health. [OR According to the findings, red wine is good for your health.]
3. This school was built 50 years ago, but still looks new.
4. Some people in the audience booed and shouted at the speaker.

QUESTION 9

Wrong sentences are indicated by an asterisk (*):

1. *He tried lifting the weight but was too heavy.
2. He tried lifting the weight but was too exhausted.
3. *He couldn't lift the weight as was too heavy.
4. *He couldn't lift the weight as was too exhausted.
5. She greeted us and sat down.
6. *She greeted us before sat down.
7. *He checked his pocket and was full of coins.
8. He checked his pocket and took out the coins.

EXPLANATION: When a sentence is joined (by a conjunction *and/but*) to another sentence, the subject of the second sentence can be left out if it is *identical* to that of the first. For example, in sentence 2: 'He tried lifting the weight but (he) was too exhausted'. But not in sentence 1: 'He tried lifting the weight but *(it) was too heavy'. In sentence 4, the second half — 'as (he) was too exhausted' — is not a sentence in its own right (i.e. it is not an 'independent clause').

QUESTION 10

From the given data, it seems that, if the subject is singular, the verb should be in the 'singular' form (with a suffix *-s* added), and if the subject is plural, the verb should be in the 'plural' form (with no suffix added).

QUESTION 11

These additional data show that the hypothesis made under Question 4 is true only for verbs in the **present tense**. In other words, generally speaking, subject-verb agreement applies *only* in the present tense. NB: There is one verb in English — the verb *be* — which obeys its own laws when it comes to agreement. Luckily, it is the *only* verb that behaves this way, so it's a simple matter of learning a few special forms:

   I <u>was</u>, we/you/they <u>were</u>, he/she/it <u>was</u>
   The student <u>is/was</u>, the students <u>are/were</u>

QUESTION 12

1. My friends <u>visit</u> me very often.
2. My best friend <u>lives</u> in the next block.
3. One of my friends <u>is</u> a disc jockey.
4. Most of our teachers <u>prefer</u> to teach in Chinese.
5. He <u>spends</u> most of his money on CDs.
6. He and his wife <u>spend</u> most of their money on CDs.
7. Many of the soldiers <u>have</u> deserted.

8. One of the soldiers <u>is</u> staying behind.
9. Each of these books <u>costs</u> more than $200.
10. Few of these books <u>cost</u> less than $250.
11. Most of the money <u>has</u> been lost.
12. Most of the furniture <u>has</u> been stolen.
13. Most of the students <u>have</u> signed up.

QUESTION 13

1. There <u>are</u> many people who would just keep quiet about it.
2. There <u>is</u> a quality which is universally admired in all cultures.
3. In the middle of the square <u>stands</u> a statue of the great leader.
4. On the shelf <u>are</u> many books on music.

QUESTION 14

The preferred answers are:
1. The committee <u>has</u> unanimously passed the motion.
2. The committee <u>are</u> very upset by the bad publicity.
3. His family <u>have</u> not spoken to him for years.
4. His family <u>is</u> the most important thing in his life.
5. The public <u>is</u> showing strong support for the new president.
6. Though the public <u>have</u> different opinions on the issue, efforts are still being made to reach a consensus.

Additional exercises

Just for interest, here are the original texts from which these exercises are constructed. You need not, of course, come up with exactly the same words, as long as your words make sense in context and observe subject-verb agreement:

EXERCISE 1

Text 1

Four men were attacked by a group of masked men wielding knives at Shamshuipo early on Thursday.

Around 12.39 am, <u>a 55-year-old man, surnamed Hui,</u> and <u>his 40-year-old friend, surnamed Lam,</u> were talking on the corner of Shek Kip Mei Street and Fuk Wa Street.

"Suddenly <u>four masked men</u> jumped out of a private car and started attacking the victims," a police spokeswoman said.

She added: "After chopping them repeatedly, the suspects fled in the private car on Boundary Road towards Kowloon City."

The victims were taken to Caritas Hospital for treatment.

Police said the victims did not know the men and had no idea why they were attacked.

Text 2

A woman and her new boyfriend were found burned alive in bed together yesterday after her former lover allegedly set light to her Tuen Mun home.

The 32-year-old suspect had allegedly got into the woman's 21st-floor flat in Castle Peak Road after climbing in through the kitchen window at about 9am.

"He allegedly poured gasoline into one of the bedrooms through the door gap when his ex-girlfriend and her boyfriend were asleep inside," a police source said.

"He set the inflammable liquid alight and then ran out of the unit through the main door."

EXERCISE 2

Text 1

There have been many articles and letters in the *South China Morning Post* about the proposed ban on smoking in restaurants.

As a teenager, not only must I endure second-hand smoke when I am out eating, but I also have to put up with it when I play sports in public playgrounds, play video games in a games centre, and when I surf the Net at Internet cafes.

I understand that a smoking ban is already in place in certain public areas, however, I see little being done to punish those who flout the regulations.

Unless the government decides to take action, for example, increasing fines for people who disobey the law, there is little point in extending the ban if smokers continue to ignore it.

Text 2

Two men have been caught using a video camera to record a preview of a film — the first arrest of its kind since an amended copyright law came into effect in April last year.

The two, aged 26 and 27, were arrested at the Broadway Theatre in Sai Yeung Choi Street, Mongkok, during a preview of the Hong Kong-made action movie *So Close* on Saturday. They were caught with a digital video camera and two cassettes.

The new film stars Taiwanese actress Shu Qi and *Shaolin Soccer*'s Karen Mok Man-wai and Vicky Zhao Wei. It centres on an international conspiracy involving murders and computer viruses.

Text 3

Cinemas <u>expect</u> attendance levels to double from today when ticket prices <u>are</u> cut to $25 for films screened on Tuesdays and Wednesdays.

Box-office takings <u>have</u> slumped to record lows this summer, diving more than 45 per cent from $386 million last year.

In July last year, the local smash hits *Shaolin Soccer* and *Love on a Diet* together grossed $90 million, but this year the biggest releases, *Men in Black II* and *Minority Report*, <u>have</u> taken only half that amount.

Unit 2: Nouns and Noun Phrases

The concept of 'number' (singular vs. plural) and of subject-verb agreement may seem fairly simple to you, but students do make lots of mistakes with it. The main part of this unit is designed not only to take you over familiar territory, but also to make you think in a new way about it. In addition to the questions, which will help you figure out the grammar for yourselves, you'll also find a certain amount of explanation. We've tried to keep this to a minimum in the units themselves, as we do not want you to rely too much on explanations, but on your *own* analytic and problem-solving skills instead.

If we think there's a need to elaborate on the simple explanations given in the units, we'll do it here in the Notes for Students. In this unit, the count/mass noun distinction may need some further explanation.

Count and mass nouns

First of all, you must bear in mind that grammatical 'explanations' are seldom completely reliable. This is because the grammar of a language is *not* the result of 'rules' made by someone at some time in the past. Grammar develops naturally over time, and though many things in it are highly *systematic* or *regular*, it is rarely as simple as black and white. The so-called explanations offered by linguists (people who analyse language scientifically) are merely attempts to *generalize* over the language phenomena that they observe. So if an explanation seems to make sense to you, and to fit (to a high degree) the language phenomena that you yourself have observed, then by all means make use of it for whatever it's worth. If not, just forget it!

The distinction given in this unit between count nouns and mass nouns (which we've borrowed from Cognitive Grammar) is based on the perceived distinction between things in this world which are *inherently bounded*, and things which are not. Take *water* and *lake*. Both words refer to things which are made up of the same substance, i.e. water. But the word *water* does not carry within itself a 'natural' or 'inherent' boundary. Sure, we can put an *arbitrary* limit on water, and say 'this much' or 'that much' water. But the point is that *water* itself is not naturally bounded. This means that *water* is infinitely expandable or contractible; it can be as little or as much as you want it, but whether it is a drop, a tankful, or an ocean of water, it is still water. *Lake*, on the other hand, is an inherently bounded body of water. It may be large or small, but the concept of a boundary is essential for it — without a boundary, there is simply no lake, and you cannot take a part of a lake and say, 'this is a lake'. Think of the relationship between other mass and count nouns — e.g. *money* vs. *dollar*, *time* vs. *hour*, and you will see a similar distinction.

The 'bounded' vs. 'unbounded' explanation will go some way towards helping you understand the 'count' vs. 'mass' noun distinction. Ultimately, the 'authority' rests with the users of the language — whether they treat a particular noun as count or mass — or as both, with a fine distinction between the different senses of the noun. When in doubt, consult a dictionary.

The introduction makes the important point that nouns in English generally require a **determiner** to indicate what objects or persons they refer to. This is especially true of **singular count nouns** — like *car, policeman, book, house*, etc. A singular count noun *must* take a determiner (*a car, the car, this car, my car*, etc.), and would be ungrammatical without one, as in: *'Car is here', *'House has been sold', etc. In this respect, English is different from Chinese, where a determiner is not needed if the 'car' or 'house' is understood (think of the equivalents of these sentences in Chinese).

In English, **singular mass nouns**, like *rice* or *water*, or **plural count nouns**, like *cars* or *houses*, do not require a determiner when used generally. When used to refer to specific objects, a determiner is used, as in '*This* rice is very good' and '*Those* cars are expensive'.

But remember that not everything can be explained with reasons. The fact is that English grammar happens to *require* a determiner to be used with singular count nouns, so remember to write '*The* car is new' or 'He has bought *a* car', instead of *'Car is new' and *'He has bought car'.

The noun phrase

For Chinese learners, the biggest problems with the noun phrase are:

(a) use of determiners
(b) plural forms of nouns
(c) modifiers that come *after* the noun instead of before it.

(c) is especially hard for learners to get used to. The difference between English and Chinese is pretty big here. Let's take the following English sentences, which contain a 'complex' noun phrase (given in square brackets):

1. [The book on the table] belongs to me.
2. [All people who love their country] should defend it with their lives.

Compare these noun phrases in English and Chinese (the noun head is in bold print, and the modifier is underlined):

ENGLISH	CHINESE
1. the **book** <u>on the table</u>	the <u>on the table</u> **book**
2. all **people** <u>who love their country</u>	all <u>love their country</u> **people**

In Chinese, all modifiers (e.g. 'on the table') come *before* the noun head (e.g. 'book'). It is easy therefore to know what the noun head is — it's always at the end of a noun phrase in Chinese. In English, only determiners and adjectives come before the noun head (e.g. 'the new book'). Other modifiers — such as **preposition phrases** (e.g. 'on the table', 'at the airport', etc.) and **relative clauses** (e.g. 'who love their country', 'which sold a million copies', etc.) must come *after* the noun head ('the book on the table', 'the book which sold a million copies'). This may make it hard for you to identify the noun head, because it may be far from the end of the noun phrase. Questions 6–7 and additional exercise 1 will give you more practice on this.

Answers to the questions are provided below. Remember that they are meant only as a check on how well you did. Learning these answers is of little value in itself — working them out is what really matters.

Suggested answers

QUESTION 1

Some examples are:

> He took *a breath of air*.
> There were *lumps of earth* on the bathroom floor.
> *A grain of sand* stuck to his nose.
> *An ounce of gold* isn't worth much these days.
> He has *loads of money* in the bank.
> She was away for *a period of time*.
> Let me offer you *a piece of advice*.
> He doesn't have *a bit of courage*.

QUESTION 2

10. *I can see <u>soldier</u> everywhere.
11. *<u>Tree</u> is essential for parks.
12. *After school, I have to read a lot of <u>book</u>.

The above nouns cannot be used here in the singular form, since the context implies a number greater than one. They should all be in the plural: *soldiers, trees, books*.

QUESTION 3

Money is a mass noun and *flower* is a count noun. The grammatical differences between the two types of nouns are:

1. Mass nouns but not count nouns can be used on their own without a determiner;
2. Count nouns but not mass nouns have a plural form;
3. Count nouns but not mass nouns can take a numerical determiner like *a*;
4. Mass nouns take the quantifiers *much/a little* while count nouns take *many/a few*.

QUESTION 4

MASS NOUNS (notice that these are all 'unbounded' entities): *water, sand, money, literature, vegetation, furniture.*

COUNT NOUNS (notice that these are all 'bounded' entities): *lake, pond, dune, dollar, cent, novel, poem, flower, tree, chair, table.*

QUESTION 5

Sentences a–d are all about the 'boy'. 'Boy' is the noun head of all the underlined noun phrases. All these noun phrases, no matter how long, can be replaced by the pronoun 'he'.

QUESTION 6

The noun heads, which control subject-verb agreement, are underlined:
1. [The **leader** of the **rebels**] has surrendered.
2. [The newly-elected **spokesman** for the **workers**] seems very inexperienced.
3. [The former **lovers** of the **president**] have come forward one by one.
4. [The **players** who lost to the **newcomer**] were taken by surprise.
5. [The **disease** which struck fear in **millions** of **people**] was SARS.

QUESTION 7

1. (The schedule showing the jetfoil arrivals and departures) is out-of-date.
2. (His book of old photographs) is missing.
3. (The recent development of new public facilities) has led to an increase in tourism in the area.
4. (The trees in the park) need trimming.
5. (The floods which hit Hunan Province recently) have caused untold damage.
6. (The search for the terrorists) goes on.
7. (The new neighbour who moved in yesterday with 11 dogs) seems a little weird.
8. (The Olympic athlete with the greatest number of gold medals) is Mark Spitz.
9. (A car with four doors) costs a little more than one with two.
10. (The mathematician whose Nobel Prize surprised many people) is John Nash.

QUESTION 8

There are several possibilities in the choice of determiners. Here are just a few:
3. I saw a/the/his car in the/a garage yesterday.
4. The/a robber shot the/a policeman outside the/a bank.
5. My/her friend works in a/this restaurant.
6. The/our teacher gave a very boring lecture today.

QUESTION 9

Basically, these nouns refer to individual objects or people (rather than objects and people in general), and determiners help to limit their reference.

QUESTION 10

(Discuss with your classmates or teacher if you have problems understanding why any of these determiners are used)

Once upon <u>a</u> time, there was <u>an</u> old man in Northern China called Yu Gong ('Foolish Old Man'). In front of <u>his</u> house stood <u>two</u> tall mountains. To go to <u>the</u> nearest town, Yu Gong had to go around <u>these</u> mountains, which took <u>a</u> long time. So <u>one</u> day he called <u>his</u> family together, and announced that they would start digging and removing <u>the</u> mountains. He said, 'When <u>my</u> sons and I are dead and gone, <u>their</u> sons will carry on, and <u>their</u> sons and <u>their</u> sons ...'

QUESTION 11

In the suggested answers below, determiners are inserted only where required by the grammar (it's all right if you've inserted other determiners which make sense, but if you left out any of the required determiners, the results would be ungrammatical):

After waiting for several years, <u>my</u> friend finally decided to buy <u>a</u> DVD-player. He waited for such <u>a</u> long time because of <u>the</u> coding system which makes _____ DVDs from _____ different parts of <u>the</u> world incompatible, which is <u>a</u> terrible nuisance. Later on, _____ DVD-players which can play all codes became available, and that solved <u>the</u> problem. He now rents and watches <u>a</u> movie every day.

QUESTION 12

I've bought <u>a</u> new car. It is <u>a</u> Mazda sports car. It has <u>a</u> slim body but <u>a</u> powerful engine. <u>The</u> engine is turbo-charged, and <u>the</u> car can accelerate from 0 to 100 kph in 5 seconds.

(i) The indefinite article *a (an)* is used when an object or person is mentioned for the first time in the context.
(ii) The definite article *the* is used when an object or person has already been mentioned earlier in the context.

QUESTION 13

I've bought <u>a</u> new car. <u>The</u> engine is turbo-charged and super powerful. <u>The</u> bumpers are made of <u>a</u> special material which can withstand <u>the</u> severest punishment. <u>The</u> seats are made of <u>the</u> best leather, and are electrically-operated.

Even when a noun has not been mentioned before in the context, the definite article can be used if it belongs to an object already mentioned. For example, when 'a new car' has already been introduced, its engine, bumpers, seats, etc. are now 'definite', since we now know which engine, bumpers or seats are referred to. Another use of the definite article is to refer to something of the 'highest degree', e.g. '*the* severest punishment' and '*the* best leather', since there's (presumably) only one highest or best.

QUESTION 14

In all these cases, the **context** makes it clear what the noun refers to. For example, in (1), when you say 'Do you have *the key*?', you are likely to be standing in front of a door (to a meeting room, office, home, or whatever), and it is obvious that you are referring to the key to that door; or a place may have been mentioned previously, e.g. someone may have said, 'Let's get it from the storeroom', and when you say 'Do you have the key?', it obviously refers to the key to the storeroom; and so on. The same goes for examples (2–4). In other examples (5, 7, 8), your location at the moment of speaking makes it clear which library (the one on the campus where you are), which manager (of the establishment where you are), which airport (of the city where you are). In (6), there is only one police force in the place where you are anyway (just as there is only one government). In (10), you would say such a thing only if you're witnessing a problem before you, so it is clear which problem you're referring to. In all cases then, you use the definite article *the* because the **context** at the time of speaking makes it perfectly clear what the noun refers to, even without any previous mention.

QUESTION 15

In all the (a) sentences, we're referring to a noun whose identity is not yet established, and so it is 'indefinite'. In (b), enough information is provided *in the rest of the sentence* to make the identity of the referent (the thing referred to) unique or unmistakable. For example, there is only one possible book referred to by (1b) '... most interesting book I have read', or (2b) '... only book on astrology in the bookstore'; and likewise only one possible referent for (3b) '... first girlfriend I ever had' and (4b) '... key to the safe in his pocket'.

QUESTION 16

The (a) sentences refer to things *in general* (e.g. children or stray dogs in general), whereas the (b) sentences, with the definite article *the*, refer to *specific* things which are understood in the present context. For example, in (1b), he loves certain specific children (understood in context as, e.g., his own children, or the children in a certain refugee camp, etc.), and not children in general. The same applies to all the other examples. (In 4b, we're talking about a particular consignment of rice, such as the one now being sold in his shop, or in his pantry.)

QUESTION 17

The missing determiners are highlighted (see p.174). Where an existing determiner is redundant, it is enclosed in square brackets [ ].

1. The majority of **the** respondents agreed.
2. Most of **the** plants were giant plants.
3. All of them agreed that **the** ability to communicate was important.
4. The vitamin can inhibit **the** development of cancer.
5. It contains **a** large amount of carotene.
6. It is used by **the** human body.
7. We should save [the] energy as much as possible.
8. The layer of [the] mud became hard rock.

Additional exercises

EXERCISE 1

1. [The first <u>anniversary</u> of the September 11 terrorist attacks] **was** commemorated all over the world.
2. [The <u>families</u> of the victims] **were** invited to attend memorial services in New York, Washington and Pennsylvania.
3. [The <u>names</u> of all those who died in the World Trade Centre] **are/were** read out by the former mayor of New York, Rudy Giuliani, and others.
4. [<u>Documentaries</u> on the attacks and their aftermath] **were** shown on TV in Hong Kong.
5. [The <u>documentary</u> which caught the attention of most viewers] **was** about a young fireman on his first job in New York.
6. [The <u>cameramen</u> who shot this documentary] **were** two French brothers.
7. [The <u>film</u> which they shot inside the World Trade Centre during the attack] **was** the only one of its kind.

EXERCISE 2

Blanks which need not be filled by a determiner are marked with <u>(X)</u>:

Text 1

<u>(X)</u> Evidence is growing of <u>a</u> link between global warming and <u>the</u> floods and droughts that devastated parts of Asia, southern Africa and Europe <u>this</u> year, <u>the</u> head of <u>the</u> United Nations' body on climate change said yesterday.

Rajendra Pachauri, chairman of the Inter-governmental Panel on Climate Change, told summit delegates there was undeniable proof that <u>the</u> Earth was warming.

"I think the evidence is becoming stronger that <u>a</u> lot of these extreme [weather] events are part of <u>the</u> overall process of climate change ... there is <u>a</u> fair amount of statistical evidence and there is certainly anecdotal evidence ... and I think <u>the</u> indications are that there is <u>a</u> link there."

Text 2

A love-struck Chinese couple handcuffed themselves to each other during a tour outing and ended up being stopped by (X) policemen after a tourist mistook them for escaped convicts and alerted the authorities.

The man, identified only as Mr Wang, had returned to Shanghai recently to visit his girlfriend.

He had been studying in (X) Japan for two years, *Shanghai Morning Post* reported. On (X) Wednesday night, the couple decided to travel to Hangzhou, the capital of Zhejiang province.

To show his deep love for her, he produced a pair of handcuffs and locked their wrists together, explaining to her that this was currently the most popular way of expressing love in Japan.

As they walked (X) hand in hand — literally — in the city, a tourist, thinking that they were (X) escaped convicts, reported them to a policeman.

Text 3

A pet shop in Hong Kong is renting out (X) puppies in an effort to find a "solution to the problem of dogs being dumped by their owners" (*South China Morning Post*, August 29).

I am opposed to this horrible rental scheme, because it will not be good for the mental health of the puppies.

Imagine having a human baby on rental. The child would be traumatized and grow up without any sense of having a permanent identity. The puppies that are rented out will be troubled in their own canine way. As they grow up they may find it difficult to respond to (X) humans. It may be good for the pet shop's business, but the proprietor should think about how it will affect the dogs mentally.

Text 4

Premier Zhu Rongji is more popular than President Jiang Zemin among (X) young Hong Kong people, a survey found yesterday — but late leaders Deng Xiaoping and Mao Zedong are admired even more.

Mr Zhu ranked fourth in the list of best leaders, with 23 votes, while Mr Jiang came 12th with only eight votes.

The survey of 502 people was conducted by the Hong Kong Federation of Youth Groups.

Topping the list was Sun Yat-sen, founder of modern China, followed by Deng Xiaoping and Mao.

Former US president Bill Clinton, at seventh, was the highest-ranking foreign leader.

The phone survey was carried out (X) last month and respondents were aged 15 to 34.

Democratic Party legislator Cheung Man-kwong said that Mr Zhu had successfully established a good image among the Hong Kong public with his determination to fight corruption on the mainland.

"It seems that Zhu is the type of leader Hong Kong people would accept," he said. Interviewees were also asked to list the qualities needed most by a good leader.

(X) Integrity was ranked top, followed by (X) credibility, management skills and ability to communicate well.

Text 5

Fixed-line phone networks were flooded with 26 million calls in an hour on Wednesday after the Observatory announced just before (X) midday that the No. 8 typhoon signal would be hoisted.

The flood of calls between midday and 1 pm was up to six times the capacity of the networks, which between them can handle only about four million calls an hour, the Office of the Telecommunications Authority (Ofta) said.

The mobile networks, which have a similar combined capacity, were flooded with 14 million calls in the same hour. There are four fixed-line operators and six mobile phone networks in the territory. Ofta secretary-general Anthony Wong Sei-kei defended the networks, saying all remained functioning and none crashed. "The reason people could not get through was because all the networks were overloaded," he said.

Unit 3: Tense and Finiteness

Verbs are the class of words in English (and in other European languages) which have the greatest number of different forms. That's because verbs carry more extra 'information' than other words, having to show finiteness/non-finiteness, tense (present/past), number (singular/plural), aspect (progressive/perfect), and voice (active/passive). But consider yourself lucky. Verbs in some other European languages have to carry even more information than in English!

By comparison, verbs in Chinese are far simpler. That's because Chinese has other ways of conveying these types of information — by using additional words (like *now* and *before*), rather than by attaching 'bits' of words (inflections like *-s* and *-ed*) to the main verb. The important thing is to know what these inflections do, and how to use them.

We have already seen how the form of a verb indicates number (by adding *-s* to the present tense form of a verb if the subject is singular). In Unit 3, we see that a verb has 6 forms, and 3 of these are used to indicate finiteness — i.e. the 'limiting' of a verb to the present or past time frame, and to a singular or plural subject (only in the present tense). This is one of the most important and basic points in English grammar: **The main verb of a sentence must be finite.**

We must add a note here on two points raised in the main part of Unit 3, concerning the forms of a verb.

Past tense vs. past participle

For some students, a lot of unnecessary confusion has arisen about **verb forms**. Most of it has to do with the fact that certain forms with different labels may actually look identical, in particular, (i) the **past tense** and **past participle** forms of most verbs, as in *talked* in (1–2) below:

1. They talked too much yesterday. (past tense *talked*)
2. They have talked too much already. (past participle *talked*)

And (ii) the **present tense (general)** and **infinitive** forms, as in *eat* in (3–4):

3. They eat a lot. (present tense *eat*)
4. They try to eat a lot. (infinitive *eat*)

First, let's take another look at the past tense and past participle forms. Consider the following sets of sentences:

5. They talk too much.
6. They talked too much yesterday.
7. They have talked too much already.
8. They eat too much.
9. They ate too much yesterday.
10. They have eaten too much already.

Now, just because the past participle form of *talk* is identical to the past tense form, some people mix the two together, and say that *talked* in sentences 6–7 are both the 'past tense' form. If you think about sentences 5–10 a little more and look at the larger picture, does this make sense? Does it really make sense to say that in 'They have talked too much already', the underlined verb is in the 'past tense' form, but in 'They have eaten too much already', it is in the 'past participle' form?

It would make more sense to say that **both** *talked* and *eaten,* **as they are used in the above contexts** (7 and 10), are in the past participle form. The fact that the past participle form of *talked* is identical to the past tense form *talked* is not a good enough reason to say that both are 'past tense', or at least 'the same' thing. By the same logic, we would not say that, just because the plural form of the noun *sheep* is also *sheep*, the two *sheep* in sentences 11–12 are the same thing, because they are clearly not:

11. The sheep is running away.
12. The sheep are running away.

The infinitive

Another confusion that needs to be cleared up is the present tense (general) form (e.g. *eat*) and the infinitive form (e.g. [*to*] *eat*), which are identical (if the *to* in the infinitive form is absent). Again, just because the two forms look the same, some people think that they are the same thing. Take the following cases:

13. They eat a lot.
14. They try to eat a lot.

It's quite easy to find out whether the two *eat* are really the same. Suppose we change the time frame to the past, or change the subject to the singular form. What will happen?

13a. They <u>ate</u> a lot yesterday.
13b. He <u>eats</u> a lot.
14a. They tried to <u>eat</u> a lot yesterday.
14b. He tries to <u>eat</u> a lot.

The *eat* in (13) changes to the past tense form *ate* in (13a) and the present tense 3rd person singular form *eats* in (13b), but the *eat* in (14) remains unchanged in (14a) and (14b). Obviously, the two *eat* in (13) and (14) are different things — in (13) it is in the present tense form, and thus changes into past tense when the time is changed, and into the 3rd person singular form when the subject is singular, whereas the *eat* in (14) is an infinitive, and is therefore *not* affected by time or number or anything else.

All this may seem a lot to say about a small thing, but it is important to establish that a verb has *six* different forms, as given in (i–vi), even though some of them may *look* the same on the surface.

'Future tense'

You may have noticed that we've not said anything about the so-called 'future tense', but only the present and past tenses. This is because we do not want to mix up **form** and **meaning**. Tense is a matter of grammatical **form**: a verb takes on a different form — e.g. having a suffix like *-s* or *-ed* attached to it — when a different tense is used. In referring to future time, the verb does not undergo any change in form. You simply use an auxiliary like *will, shall, may,* etc. before the verb. So 'future' is not really a 'tense' in English. Future time is a matter of *meaning*, not *form*.

Another reason why we do not refer to *will rain* etc. as 'future tense' is that *will* does not specially mark future time. *All* the **modal auxiliaries** (*will, shall, must, may, can*) refer to future time. For example:

1. It <u>will rain</u> tomorrow.
2. It <u>may rain</u> tomorrow.
3. Anything <u>can happen</u> tomorrow.
4. The tenant <u>must move out</u> tomorrow.
5. We <u>shall move out</u> tomorrow.

All the above auxiliaries refer to future time, and differ among themselves only with respect to the degree of **likelihood** or force. Therefore, it is not very logical to label *will* alone as marking the 'future tense'.

The important thing is to know how to use the above auxiliaries, plus other constructions like *be going to* ('He is going to move out tomorrow'), and the present tense ('The offer ends tomorrow'), to refer to future time.

Suggested answers

QUESTION 1

One form only — 吃

QUESTION 2

Eat, eats, eating, ate, eaten

QUESTION 3

	wash	break	run	hear
Present tense (general)	wash	break	run	hear
Present tense (3rd per. sing.)	washes	breaks	runs	hears
Past tense	washed	broke	ran	heard
Present participle	washing	breaking	running	hearing
Past participle	washed	broken	run	heard
Infinitive *(to)*	wash	break	run	hear

Non-finite forms: Just an additional note. Being non-finite, the forms *(to) eat, eating* and *eaten* are not 'limited' to any time frame or subject. Thus, they can refer to both past and present and both singular and plural, as shown in the following examples, where the non-finite forms don't change even when the finite forms change their tenses:

1. I begged him to eat.
2. I'm begging you to eat.
3. I caught them eating my chocolates.
4. Don't let me catch you eating my chocolates.
5. He found the carcass eaten by crocodiles.
6. You will find all the food eaten by the kids.

QUESTION 4

1. He lived in Hong Kong when he was a child. Now he lives in Singapore.
2. In 1950, a domestic maid earned about $50 a month; now she earns $3,600.
   (For [1] and [2] *lived, earned* and *was* are limited to past time and *was* to a singular subject, and *lives* and *earns* are limited to present time and a singular subject.)
3. When he arrived home last night, he found the door broken, so he called the police.
   (All the above past tense verbs are limited to past time.)
4. Whenever he has time, he swims and jogs to stay in shape.
   (All the above present tense verbs are limited to present time and a singular subject.)

5. Though the last plane has left, many people are still waiting for a flight out.
   (*Has* is limited to present time and a singular subject, and *are* to present time and a plural subject.)
6. He did not report for work yesterday as he was not feeling well.
   (*Did* and *was* are limited to past time, and *was* to a singular subject.)

QUESTION 5

Notice that only **finite** forms of verbs can fill these blanks, as they are the main verb of the sentence.

1. He saw the new James Bond movie last week.
2. She writes/wrote letters to her parents very often.
3. He broke the door with his hands.
4. Tom heard the news on the radio.
5. He eats/ate nothing but boiled vegetables.
6. He lives/lived in Repulse Bay, but his wife lives/lived in Ma On Shan.

QUESTION 6

1. Half of the respondents [being] **were/are** neutral with that question.
2. Millions of years ago, some of the lands [become] **became** seas, and some [becomes] **became** rivers.
3. The vegetation was covered by a layer of mud which [consist] **consisted** of sand and small rocks.
4. I went to the park and [watch] **watched** the kids play football.

QUESTION 7

The examples clearly show that only the *first* verb in a verb group can be marked for tense.

QUESTION 8

1. Would Kevin [stopped] **stop** seeing his friends?
   (*Would stop* is a verb group, and only the first verb *would* can have tense.)
2. She can't [tolerated] **tolerate** such an unreliable relationship.
   (*Can't tolerate* is a verb group, and only the first verb can have tense.)
3. More than 50% did not [agreed] **agree** with that.
   (*Did* [*not*] *agree* is a verb group, and only the first verb can have tense.)
4. She can't be bothered with all these details.
   (This is correct. *Bothered* is the past participle form used to show **passive voice**, not tense.)
5. He did not wash the dishes last night. (Correct.)
6. He **is** always playing in the field.
   (*Playing* alone is non-finite, so we need the finite form *is playing*.)

7. The window **was** broken by someone yesterday.
   (*Broken* alone is non-finite, so we need the finite form *was broken*.)
8. When I phoned him last night, he **was** having a shower.
   (*Having* alone is non-finite, and requires the finite form *was having*.)

QUESTION 9

In sentences 1–5, the verb is the *second* verb in a verb group (though separated from the first verb), and so should be in the non-finite form. In sentence 8, *to buy* has an infinitive marker *to*.

1. Though I asked him many times, he would not <u>tell</u> me the answer.
2. When the bill came, he suddenly realized that he did not <u>have</u> enough money.
3. Do you think he should <u>apologize</u> for what he said?
4. How could he possibly <u>know</u> what we were planning?
5. I did not deliberately <u>step</u> on your toes.
6. Whenever it rains, the temperature always <u>drops</u>.
7. When the enemy advanced, they <u>retreated</u>, and when the enemy retreated, they <u>advanced</u>.
8. His wife told him to <u>buy</u> a watermelon, but he <u>bought</u> a durian instead.
9. Though he is very rich, he never <u>shows</u> it.
10. Though he was poor, he <u>pretended</u> to be rich.

QUESTION 10

Sentences 1–4 show that the present tense ('simple present') is used for an 'activity' verb (*play, deliver*, etc.) which stands for a *repeated* activity in the present time frame. Notice that it does *not* have to be a frequent or regular activity (as some people think), as shown in (2) and (4). The point is that it is not a single event but a repeated event, whether many times or just a few times. The time frame is the *general* present, not the present moment (the moment of speaking).

Sentences 5–8 show that the present tense is used for 'state' verbs (like *live, know*), to indicate a stable state that extends over the present time frame. It may of course change in the future, but it is true at present and is assumed to go on for an indefinite period.

QUESTION 11

The verbs in these examples refer to *timeless* facts. So they are true in the past, present and future.

QUESTION 12

These activities are all in the future (usually near, but not necessarily) — the important thing being that they are all known in advance to happen at a chosen time, usually because it is planned that way.

QUESTION 13

These events all happen at the precise moment of speaking. In fact, the very act of *speaking* makes it happen! Notice that they all involve the first person pronoun (*I*, or *we* in other cases), for obvious reasons.

QUESTION 14

In 1, 4 and 7, where the present tense is used, the condition (e.g. 'if I hear anything') is a perfectly possible one.

In 2, 5 and 9, in the past tense, the condition (e.g. 'if I had a million dollars') is either impossible, or very unlikely. Using the past tense makes the condition more 'distant' from present reality, but it has nothing to do with past time.

In 3, 6 and 8, in the past perfect, we're referring to a past situation: the condition ('if I had ... etc.') is something that did not actually happen in the past, but it was possible and *could have happened*, and you're imagining the result if it had happened.

QUESTION 15

1. Luckily it stopped raining two days ago. If the rain <u>does not stop/did not stop</u>/**had not stopped**, the town <u>will be flooded/would be flooded</u>/**would have been flooded**.
2. I'm going to the bookstore this afternoon. If **I find**/<u>found/had found the book</u>, I **will get**/<u>would get/would have got</u> it for you.
3. If I <u>am</u>/**were**/<u>had been</u> your father, I <u>will spank</u>/**would spank**/<u>would have spanked</u> you, but I'm only your teacher.
4. The police are out looking for the terrorist. If they **find** him, they **will shoot** him on sight.
5. The police surrounded the terrorists' hideout but failed to catch anyone. If they **had caught** some of the terrorists, the police chief **would have been** very proud of them.
6. Unfortunately, he doesn't exercise or play any sports. If he **did**, he **would not be** as fat as he is.

Additional exercises

EXERCISE 1

The finite verbs are marked [F] and the non-finite verbs [NF]:

There <u>is</u> [F] something about <u>lying</u> [NF] on your back in a hospital bed with half a dozen needles <u>poking</u> [NF] out of your skin that <u>makes</u> [F] you really <u>ponder</u> [NF] your health, and how to <u>maintain</u> [NF] it.

The sound of the old man in the next bed <u>snoring</u> [NF] loudly <u>is</u> [F] testament to just how relaxing acupuncture really <u>can be</u> [F]. But <u>being</u> [NF] the youngest patient in the clinic by at least two generations <u>did make</u> [F] me <u>wonder</u> [NF] whether acupuncture and its associated traditional therapies <u>are</u> [F] strictly for the old.

EXERCISE 2

Text 1

A passenger <u>told</u> yesterday of frightening scenes aboard the holiday cruise ship *SuperStar Leo* when it <u>ran</u> into severe tropical storm Hagupit on Wednesday, forcing it to <u>change</u> course and <u>return</u> to Hong Kong a day late.

Passengers <u>were</u> slammed against walls, tables <u>overturned</u> and luggage <u>fell</u> from overhead lockers, the passenger said.

The vessel's operator, *Star Cruises*, <u>confirmed</u> the day-long delay <u>was</u> caused by the closure of Hong Kong harbour, which <u>forced</u> *Leo* to <u>seek</u> shelter near Dangan Island, about 30 km south of Tsing Yi in mainland waters. However, the company <u>denied</u> anyone <u>had</u> been injured.

The passenger said weather conditions <u>deteriorated</u> quickly after 1 pm on Wednesday and the ship <u>was</u> rocked heavily until after 5 pm. Leo <u>was</u> scheduled to return to Ocean Terminal at 4 pm on Wednesday but eventually <u>returned</u> to Hong Kong at 10 am on Thursday.

Text 2

Father Franco Mella <u>will be putting</u> even more weight behind the right-of-abode seekers after his return from a four-month visit home to Italy — where he <u>piled</u> on 10 kg.

The 53-year-old, who <u>will</u> begin a hunger strike next Monday to promote the right-of-abode cause, <u>said</u> the homemade pasta, pizza and salami served up by his 79-year-old mother <u>were</u> behind his expanded waistline.

The priest, who now <u>weighs</u> about 95 kg, <u>pointed</u> out that he <u>lost</u> about 10 kg when he <u>staged</u> a 10-day hunger strike with the abode seekers last April before returning to his home in Italy.

"When my mother first <u>saw</u> me, she <u>asked</u> me never to fast again. But when she later <u>saw</u> me becoming fatter and fatter, she <u>said</u>: 'You better go back to Hong Kong'," Father Mella said.

Unit 4: Auxiliary Verbs and Aspect

This unit is about the uses of **primary auxiliaries** in English (*be, have, do*), mainly in connection with the **progressive aspect** and **perfect aspect.** It is important to note that 'aspect' is *not* the same as 'tense'. It does not relate to present or past time as such, but to how an event is *viewed* — whether as something ongoing and incomplete (progressive aspect), or something completed (perfect aspect). The time itself may be present or past — present as in sentences 1–2, where the first verb is marked by the present tense:

1. My neighbour *is walking* his dog. (ongoing at the present moment)
2. He *has bought* a Jack Russell. (completed before the present moment)

or past, as in (3–4), where the first verb is marked by the past tense:

3. My neighbour *was walking* his dog. (ongoing at some point of time in the past)
4. He *had bought* a Jack Russell. (completed before some point of time in the past)

Notice that **tense-marking** is separate from **aspect-marking** — that's why we can contrast (i) the same tense with different aspects, e.g. *is walking* vs. *has walked*; and (ii) the same aspect with different tenses, e.g. *is walking* vs. *was walking*. The progressive or perfect aspect can combine with either the present or past tense, and vice versa.

The concept of 'aspect' is probably easier for you to grasp than 'tense', because aspect can also be found in Chinese. In Chinese, progressive aspect is marked by *zai* (在) before the verb, and perfect aspect by *le* (了) after the verb, e.g.

5. *ta zai xi che* (他在洗車)
6. *ta xi le che* (他洗了車)

(You can supply the Cantonese equivalents for the above sentences yourself.) Of course, aspect in English is more complicated than in Chinese, because it is combined with tense, so that you get 'present + progressive', 'past + progressive', 'present + perfect', and 'past + perfect'. But as long as you try to keep the two things — tense and aspect — separate in your mind (as we have tried to do in this unit), it shouldn't be too confusing.

Suggested answers

QUESTION 1

All the examples in the 'present progressive' (2, 4, 6, 8) here are about events or states which are going on at the present moment.

QUESTION 2

The present progressive here also indicates events or states which are ongoing at present, but in a broad rather than narrow sense, such that the event does not *literally* have to be going on at this very moment. For example in (2), 'She *is writing* a book on Leslie Cheung at the moment', she does not literally have to be writing or typing the book at this very moment (she may well be shopping or playing tennis right now!) But the idea is that she is currently engaged in writing such a book. The idea of *temporariness* is central in this use of the progressive aspect.

QUESTION 3

Here the progressive aspect is used for *planned* future events.

Notes and Answer Key 185

QUESTION 4

The ungrammatical ones are marked by *:

1. * I *am knowing* five languages.
2. * He *is having* a house and a car.
3. * She *is liking* classical music.
4. * This book *is belonging to me*.
5. * I *am understanding* your problem.
6. They *are thinking* about the problem.

QUESTION 5

Broadly speaking, the same types of verbs in Chinese as in English cannot take the progressive aspect, i.e. *zhidao* (知道), *you* (有), *xihuan* (喜歡), *shuyu* (屬於), *mingbai* (明白).

QUESTION 6

The verbs in Questions 4 and 5 all refer to stable, long-lasting states. Therefore, they cannot be used with progressive aspect, which implies a temporary state or activity. Note the difference between 'He *lives* with his parents' and 'He *is living* with his parents'. The first implies that this is a normal, long-term arrangement, while the second implies that it is temporary.

QUESTION 7

All these verbs have at least two senses, one referring to a stable state, and the other to a temporary, bounded activity. Only in the second sense can the verb take progressive aspect, for reasons already explained.

1. * He *is having* a sports car. (*have* = 'own', a stable state)
2. He *is having* his dinner. (*have* = 'eat', a temporary, bounded activity)
3. * He *is seeing* the picture on the wall. (*see* = 'perceive with the eyes')
4. The doctor *is seeing* his patients in the surgery. (*see* = 'treat patients')
5. * This book *is costing* $100. (*cost* = 'has the price of')
6. I must resign from the club. It *is costing* me too much. (*cost* = 'make me pay')

QUESTION 8

The past progressive indicates that an activity (e.g. he was having a shower in sentence 1) was going on at some point of time in the past (e.g. the time when I rang).

QUESTION 9

You may have your own explanations for these mistakes. One possibility is that the writer is using the auxiliary *be (am, is, are, was, were)* totally unnecessarily. But there is another possibility. Perhaps the writer is trying to give more emphasis to the sentence by using *be*. If so, he is probably using *be* like the Chinese *shi* (是) (or Cantonese '係'), where '我是 (係) 同意你的意見' is more emphatic than 'I agree with you'. But in English, the proper auxiliary to use for emphasis is **not** *be*, but *do*: 'I *do agree* with you' and 'I *do* strongly *recommend* this book'. But even then, don't use *do* for emphasis too much.

Another possible error is to use the past tense form of *be* (*was/were*) to 'double-mark' the past tense of the main verb, which is totally unnecessary, as in * 'We *were asked* 30 chief executives'.

QUESTION 10

In all these sentences, where the present perfect is used for an event (e.g. 'have eaten two pizzas'), we're viewing the event from the *end point*, when it is already completed.

QUESTION 11

In all these examples, something did not just happen in the past. Rather, some event (e.g. the plane leaving) happened *before* some other mentioned time or event in the past (e.g. the time I arrived). The use of the past perfect (e.g. 'the plane **had left**') shows that the earlier event happened before the later event ('the time I **arrived**').

QUESTION 12

The sentences where the past perfect is wrongly used are sentences 1a and 2b. In these examples, something just happened in the past, without any indication that it happened before something else; in fact, the time when it happened is even mentioned ('yesterday' or 'August 1945'). In such cases, just use the simple past tense instead of the past perfect.

QUESTION 13

1. After more than 150 years of colonial rule, Hong Kong reverted to China on July 1, 1997. By that time, it had grown from a barren rock to one of the most modern and prosperous cities in the world, and the population had increased from a few hundred to six million. After 1997, many of the people who had migrated (migrate) overseas earlier began (begin) to return, as they had found that things were not so bad after all.
2. Recently, I returned to my old neighbourhood to look for my childhood friend. I found that she had moved out long ago. Some neighbours told me that she had married a rich old man from America, and others that she had joined the sisterhood and gone to serve in India. Someone even said that she had died. I hope that I can find her again some day.

QUESTION 14

These examples show one of the differences between the past tense and the present perfect. The past tense, but not the present perfect, should be used if the time of occurrence (e.g.

'1900', '2 minutes ago') is given. The present perfect, but not the past tense, should be used if a period of time extending from the past to the present (e.g. 'since 1989', 'until now') is mentioned.

QUESTION 15

In the following contexts, sentences 1, 3, 5, 7, which use the present perfect, are more appropriate than the ones using the past tense: [NB: Sentences marked with a '?' are less appropriate.]

1. A: Can we start the party now? B: Sure, my parents *have left*.
2. ? A: Can we start the party now? B: Sure, my parents *left*.
3. The guests *have arrived*. Bring out the food.
4. ? The guests *arrived*. Bring out the food.
5. A: Would you like to join us for dinner? B: No thank you, I *have eaten*.
6. ? A: Would you like to join us for dinner? B: No thank you, I *ate*.
7. Can you give me a lift home? The last bus *has left*.
8. ? Can you give me a lift home? The last bus *left*.

The reason is that the present perfect implies *relevance* to the present. And in all the above cases, the part which is in the present perfect is very relevant to the context (e.g. because my parents have left, we can start the party now).

QUESTION 16

The verb in the present perfect (e.g. 'have written a novel') implies completion. So sentence 1 implies that the novel is finished. The verb in the present perfect progressive (e.g. 'have been writing a novel') implies that the event has been going on for some time up to the present, but is not necessarily finished.

QUESTION 17

When a main verb (e.g. *know*) is used without an auxiliary (like *be, have, will,* etc.), then the 'dummy' auxiliary *do* is needed if we turn the sentence into a question (e.g. 'Do you know ... ?', 'Why did he climb ... ?'), or a negative ('I do not know ... ').

Additional exercises

Text 1

Global economic growth <u>is taking</u> its toll on the environment, and Hong Kong's pollution is certainly the worst I <u>have seen</u>. The warning bells <u>have rung</u> and the air pollution index (API) readings keep increasing in Hong Kong. Strict policies and fines <u>have been put</u> in place, and it is well-known that the removal of lead from petrol and the use of energy-efficient technology can also greatly reduce the problems. But why <u>hasn't</u> the situation <u>improved</u>? Can't the government do more to fight pollution?

It may be our fault. Many environmental measures <u>have been set</u>, but only a few people support them. How can the air improve without our support?

The government should strictly punish people who throw rubbish on the streets or in the sea. Industries which <u>are polluting</u> our rivers and oceans must be hit with heavy fines.

Text 2

Under Article 23 of the Basic Law, Hong Kong is required to pass laws against acts of treason, secession, sedition, subversion and the theft of state secrets.

There <u>have</u> long <u>been</u> concerns that the laws will restrict freedoms and be used to clamp down on dissent.

Officials both in Hong Kong and on the mainland <u>have sought</u> to play down the fears, while insisting that the time <u>has come</u> for the national security laws to be enacted. The government is expected to release a consultation paper soon, perhaps as early as next month.

Text 3

Since the downfall of former strongman Suharto in 1998, restrictions on Chinese culture <u>have begun</u> to lift.

Last year, President Megawati <u>declared</u> Lunar New Year or *Imlek* as a national holiday, making it the first time that Chinese culture <u>had been recognized</u> officially since the 1965 ban.

Since 1999, Chinese Indonesians <u>have celebrated</u> *Imlek* openly, shopping malls <u>have been decked</u> out in red and gold lanterns every New Year, several Chinese-language newspapers <u>have hit</u> the streets, and Metro television station broadcasts the news several times a day in Putonghua.

But Hendrawan says, in practice, that many of the old laws discriminating against ethnic Chinese <u>are</u> still <u>operating</u>. Along with 100 other ethnic Chinese professionals, he <u>was meeting</u> the president's husband, Taufiq Kiemas, last night, to demand equal rights for Chinese-Indonesians.

Unit 5: Transitivity and Passive Voice

The **transitive** vs. **intransitive** distinction in **verbs** is an important one in both English and Chinese. The grammatical 'rule' itself is simple enough:

- A **transitive verb** *needs* an **object** (e.g. 'The teacher *praised* the student' vs. * 'The teacher *praised*')
- An **intransitive verb** *cannot* take an **object** (e.g. 'The teacher *smiled*' vs. * 'The teacher *smiled* the student')

But it is not easy to explain the idea behind this rule. Why should transitive and intransitive verbs behave this way?

The following explanation may be of some help to you. But remember that, just as in the case of the other 'explanations' (for count/mass nouns, finite/non-finite verb forms, etc.), it is just an attempt to help you make sense of something that would otherwise seem pretty arbitrary or mechanical. A lot of things in grammar do make sense, but not in an absolutely clear-cut way.

Intransitive verbs

Think of the activities or events that happen in real life. Some of them involve only **one (central) participant**. If you 'run' (meaning to use your legs to propel yourself), you do the running all by yourself. You don't run somebody else, nor does somebody else run you — you just move your own legs and run. (Of course, you may run *with* someone else, but that's a different matter.) The same with jogging, swimming, crawling, smiling, laughing, crying, sneezing, snoring, sleeping, standing, sitting, living, dying, etc. All these activities, which involve just one central participant, are typically represented by **intransitive verbs**, which involve only a **subject** but no **object** (which would represent a second participant in the event).

Transitive verbs

More often than not, however, an activity may involve **two** (or more) **central participants**. Think of the activity of 'hitting'. It always involves two participants: (i) a 'hitter', and (ii) somebody or something which is 'hit'. Furthermore, the activity can be said to be started by one participant (in this case the 'agent' of the hitting, i.e. the hitter), and is directed at the other participant (the 'target' or 'object' of the hitting). You'll find the same thing with other activities like touching, striking, killing, wounding, kissing, loving, hating, scolding, praising, criticizing, attacking, buying, selling, building, eating, drinking, destroying, protecting, betraying, etc. etc. They all involve at least two central participants (NB: a 'participant' need not be a living thing — e.g. a typhoon and a house can be the two participants of 'destroy', as in 'The typhoon destroyed the house'.) In terms of grammar, this sort of activity is typically represented by a **transitive verb**. A transitive verb involves both a **subject** and an **object**, which correspond to the 'agent' and the 'target' respectively.

Just two further notes. Some actions may involve *three* central participants. For example, the action of 'giving' involves (i) a 'giver', (ii) some object which is 'given', and (iii) a 'recipient' who receives the object. We call (iii) an 'indirect object'. Secondly, sometimes an object can be left out if it is commonly understood. When we say 'He's eating', we understand that he's eating some food.

Suggested answers

QUESTION 1

'Group A' verbs *slept, smiled* and *died* do not carry objects. However, 'Group B' verbs *built, damaged* and *scolded* carry objects.

QUESTION 2

When verbs like *sleep, smile* and *die* take objects, as in sentences 7, 9 and 11, the results are ungrammatical. This means that these verbs **cannot** take objects. On the other hand, when verbs like *build, damage* and *scold* are used without objects, the results too are ungrammatical. This means that such verbs **need** objects.

QUESTION 3

There are many possibilities here. Please refer to the explanations on intransitive and transitive verbs above.

QUESTION 4

You'll find that the same verbs in Chinese take objects or do not take objects. For example, 睡覺 (sleep) can't take an object. '他睡覺' is fine but *'他睡覺他的朋友' (*He slept his friend) is not. On the other hand, '建' needs an object: for example, '他建房子' is fine but not *'他建'.

QUESTION 5

The underlined phrases in sentences 2, 4, 6 and 8 are objects; those in sentences 1, 3, 5, and 7 are not. One important difference is that objects are normally **noun phrases**, like *the floor*, and not prepositional phrases, like *on the floor*.

QUESTION 6

The underlined phrases in sentences 1, 3 and 5 are objects; the others are not. One important difference is that the sentences with real objects can be turned into passive sentences, e.g. (5) 'An English teacher was hired by him', but not those without objects, e.g. (6) * 'An English teacher was become by her'.

QUESTION 7

Only sentences 1, 3 and 5 can be turned into the passive voice because they have objects:
  3. His suitcase was packed (by him) the night before the trip.
  5. An English teacher was hired by him.

QUESTION 8

1. * 'The figure *raises*.' *Raise* is a transitive verb, and requires an object, but here there's no object. What we need is an intransitive verb here, such as *rises*.
2. * 'The financial crisis *deteriorated* the economy of Hong Kong'. *Deteriorate* is an intransitive verb and cannot take an object (and here it wrongly has an object 'the economy of Hong Kong'). We'll have to say 'The economy of Hong Kong *deteriorated* because of the financial crisis', which has no object.
3. * 'The employees want the boss to *rise* their salaries.' *Rise* is an intransitive verb and cannot take an object (such as 'their salaries'). What we need is a transitive verb here, such as *raise*.

When in doubt about whether a verb used in a certain sense is transitive or intransitive, look it up in a dictionary. It will tell you where the verb is [T] (transitive) or [I] (intransitive) for a given meaning.

QUESTION 9

1. He flew from Hong Kong to San Francisco, then drove to Yosemite. INTRANSITIVE *flew*, = 'to travel by air'.
2. He flew an old plane and nearly had a crash. TRANSITIVE *flew*, = 'to operate', object: *an old plane*.
3. She walked to school yesterday as the weather was fine. INTRANSITIVE *walk*, = 'to travel on foot'.
4. She walks her dog every morning before going to school. TRANSITIVE *walk*, = 'to take for a walk', object: *her dog*.
5. He drinks tea but not coffee. TRANSITIVE *drink*, = 'to consume', object: *tea*.
6. He drinks with his friends every weekend. INTRANSITIVE *drink*, = 'to consume alcohol'.
7. Tom painted the fence all by himself. TRANSITIVE *paint*, = 'to put paint on', object: *the fence*.
8. Do you know that Tom can paint? INTRANSITIVE *paint*, = 'to paint pictures'.
9. You don't have to run every time your boss calls. INTRANSITIVE *run*, = 'to rush'.
10. The boss runs his company like a military establishment. TRANSITIVE *run*, = 'to organize and operate', object: *his company*.

QUESTION 10

You will probably find that whether we decide to include the 'agent' or 'doer' of the action ('by so-and-so') depends not only on whether we know the identity of that person, but also (if we know the identity) on whether it is informative or relevant to mention it.

1. President Kennedy was assassinated by Lee Harvey Oswald in 1963.
2. Paper was invented in China thousands of years ago. (There's no point mentioning 'by somebody' since it doesn't tell us anything really.)

3. All living things can be divided into two main types. (There's no point mentioning 'by us' since it is a general 'us' and doesn't refer to any group of people in particular.)
4. The Bank of China building in Hong Kong was designed by I. M. Pei. (Very important to mention 'by I. M. Pei', for otherwise the sentence would tell us next to nothing.)
5. My friend was kidnapped by extraterrestrial aliens and taken up into their spaceship last night. (Important to mention 'by extraterrestrial aliens', as it is a very noteworthy piece of information.)
6. The kidnappers have finally been arrested (by the police). ('By the police' can be left out if you wish, as 'arrested' already implies the police.)

QUESTION 11

1. * This vitamin can find in carrots. (The writer failed to use the passive 'This vitamin can be found in carrots'. He probably thought in terms of a topic 'this vitamin', followed by a comment '(we) can find (it) in carrots', but that is not acceptable in English.)
2. * It cannot produce by the body. (Similar comments as sentence 1. 'It cannot be produced by the body.')
3. * These results can classify three types. (Similar comments as sentence 1. 'These results can be classified into three types.')
4. * Some giant plants were decay. (Use 'decayed' or 'were decayed'. The writer seems aware of the passive, but used the wrong form of the verb *decay*.)

QUESTION 13

1. After working for 10 years as a clerk, John hopes <u>to be promoted</u>.
2. Students who are more than 15 minutes late for class <u>are treated</u> as absent.
3. When he arrived home, he noticed that all the lights <u>were switched on</u>.
4. It is very humiliating to <u>be made</u> fun of by your classmates.
5. At the time the lawyer arrived at the police station, his client <u>was being interrogated</u>.
6. In my opinion, all computer hackers <u>should be locked up</u>.
7. These diseases <u>are spread</u> by physical contact, not through the air.
8. Do you know which films <u>will be nominated</u> for next year's Academy Awards?
9. At the Asian Games, two of Hong Kong's table tennis players <u>were sent</u> home.
10. We are not sure how he died. He <u>may have been poisoned</u> (poison), or he <u>may have been shot</u>.

QUESTION 14

1. The <u>hunting</u> party rested after a long day. ('party' is the logical **subject** of 'hunt' – i.e. the party hunted somebody or something)
2. The <u>hunted</u> animals had no rest. ('animals' is the logical **object** of 'hunt' – i.e. the animals were hunted by somebody)
3. The <u>winning</u> team celebrated their victory. ('team' is subject of 'win')
4. The <u>defeated</u> team broke down in tears. ('team' is object of 'defeat')
5. The <u>crying</u> baby kept me awake all night. ('baby' is subject of 'cry')

6. There's no use crying over <u>spilled</u> milk ('milk' is object of 'spill')
7. The <u>disappointing</u> Vanessa Mae concert left a bad impression. ('concert' is subject of 'disappoint')
8. Her <u>disappointed</u> fans demanded their money back. ('fans' is object of 'disappoint')
9. The <u>exhausting</u> match lasted for five hours. ('match' is subject of 'exhaust')
10. The <u>exhausted</u> players collapsed as soon as it ended. ('players' is object of 'exhaust')

GENERALIZATION: When the **present participle** form of a verb (e.g. 'hunting') is used as an adjective before a noun, then the **noun** is normally the logical **subject** of the **verb** (e.g. the 'party' of people were the ones who did the hunting). When the **past participle** form of a verb (e.g. 'hunted') is used this way, then the noun is normally the logical **object** of the verb (e.g. the 'animals' were the ones who were hunted by the hunting party).

QUESTION 15

(The mistakes are marked with *)
1. * It was useful to study the <u>remained</u> parts of the plants. — <u>the remaining parts</u> (i.e. the parts that remain)
2. * A survey <u>conducting</u> among 100 chief executives has been published. — <u>a survey conducted</u> ... (i.e. a survey which was conducted by somebody)
3. * A million years ago, there were many giant plants <u>grown</u> on the Earth. — <u>many giant plants growing</u> (i.e. the plants were growing on the Earth)
4. * Their performance is really <u>fascinated</u>. I have seen it three times. — <u>fascinating</u> (the performance fascinates people)
5. * I was so <u>boring</u> with the math lesson that I went to sleep. — <u>bored</u> (I was bored by the math lesson)
6. These confusing rules are impossible to understand. — **Correct** (the rules confuse people, so these rules are 'confusing')
7. * The children seem <u>delighting</u> by the cartoon. — <u>delighted</u> (the children are delighted by something)
8. * The little girl was <u>frightening</u> by the fierce barking dog. — <u>frightened</u> (the dog frightened the girl)
9. The manager apologized to the annoyed customers. — **Correct** (the customers were annoyed by something)
10. The moving vehicle smashed into his rear. — **Correct**.

Additional exercises

Text 1

The disruption of the Google search engine this month appears to have been only one symptom of a significant change in the way China censors the Internet. Observers say the main focus of the so-called Great Firewall has switched from preventing access to a long list of <u>banned</u> Websites to screening Internet traffic, including e-mail, by searching out keywords and blocking the data they <u>are associated</u> with.

A far greater amount of online information <u>is denied</u> to mainland residents than was previously the case.

The changes, which began to <u>be noticed</u> around September 13, are also proving highly unpopular with many of the country's 46 million Internet users.

News sites, including the *South China Morning Post*'s scmp.com, particularly <u>are affected</u>. Mainland users can still reach the scmp.com homepage, but if they try to read stories on topics Beijing considers politically sensitive, they <u>will be blocked</u>. Even sites that offer seemingly benign information <u>are tampered</u> with.

After being off-line for two weeks this month, Google now works when users put in most words. But looking for information on a banned topic can cause searches to <u>be blocked</u> (block) until the browser <u>is restarted</u>.

Text 2

Police are considering laying charges after a Chinese flag <u>was set</u> on fire during a National Day protest yesterday.

It would be the first time that a flag-burning prosecution <u>has been brought</u> — although there have been five convictions for desecrating the national or SAR flags, the charge which could apply to the new case. In the previous cases, flags <u>were defaced</u> or <u>altered</u> by protesters.

Yesterday's flag-burning <u>happened</u> when 10 members of the April 5th Action Group marched from the Southorn Centre in Wan Chai about 7 am. A dozen police officers <u>escorted</u> the group but stopped it near Central Plaza and asked to check what was inside the coffin. They <u>demanded</u> that the protesters move to a demonstration area set up by the police.

A minor scuffle broke out as the activists defied police demands and <u>insisted</u> on heading for the waterfront. During the confusion, a national flag <u>was set</u> alight. Officers <u>used</u> a fire extinguisher to put out the blaze.

Ng Po-keung, the assistant Wan Chai division commander, said the protesters might have breached the National Flag Ordinance by burning the flag. "We will investigate the incident of burning the national flag and seek legal advice from the Justice Department as to what follow up action should <u>be taken</u>," he said.

"Long Hair" Leung Kwok-hung, a core member of the April 5th Action Group, said he was not <u>involved</u> in burning the flag.

Leung, who is on trial over unlawful assembly charges, <u>was fined</u> $6,000 for desecrating the Hong Kong flag with his colleague Koo Sze-yiu during an anti-police rally in May last year.

Text 3

Legislators and tourism industry leaders last night demanded an inquiry after thousands of Hong Kong residents and tourists <u>were stranded</u> at the Lowu border crossing because of a mainland computer breakdown.

Long queues formed on the mainland side when the crash happened at noon. It <u>took</u> 45 minutes to fix the glitch, but some people said they <u>were delayed</u> by up to two hours because of the knock-on effects.

It was an embarrassment for Shenzhen border authorities who, in response to complaints about border delays, had claimed just five weeks ago that their efficiency was "even better" than that of their Hong Kong counterparts.

About 2,000 people travelling to Shenzhen were stranded on the Lowu bridge at the peak of the hold-up. Many more had to wait on the other side of the bridge to get into Hong Kong.

Many transit passengers were angry. "I have a plane to catch. What am I supposed to do?" shouted Cheung Wai-kuen, who said he had been trapped for 30 minutes and had less than an hour to reach Shenzhen's airport.

Tony Law Yau-tong, the border commander of the Immigration Department, said some travel agents should be held responsible for the border congestion. He said only 173 mainland tour groups had told Shenzhen border authorities of visits in advance but 250 groups turned up at Lowu yesterday.

"Most of the mainland tourists are only on a short trip to Hong Kong. It must be very frustrating if most of their time is spent on queueing up for border-crossing. With the bad experience, they may not want to visit Hong Kong again," Mr Li said.

Text 4

Canto-pop star Nicholas Tse Ting-fung will be spending two weeks in jail while awaiting sentence after being convicted of perverting the course of justice on Wednesday afternoon.

The Western Court ruled that the teen idol and 28-year-old police constable Lau Chi-wai were both guilty of allowing Tse's former chauffeur, Shing Kwok-ting, to stand in as the driver of Tse's black Ferrari when it crashed at Cotton Tree Drive on March 23.

No sentence was handed down but Tse and Lau have been remanded in custody, without bail, until October 16.

Last month Shing — who was sentenced to four months' imprisonment after admitting to falsely representing himself as the driver — testified in court, under immunity for prosecution, that he had asked Tse to leave the scene of the accident.

After saying he would deal with the matter, Shing asked Constable Lau if he could stand in as driver of the vehicle. Lau allegedly agreed to the request, the court was told.

Unit 6: Verb Complementation

The idea behind '**complements**' in grammar is that not all verbs can stand alone — many of them need to be 'completed' by other words or phrases, such as objects, other verbs, clauses, etc. This is a fairly complex area, and in this unit we have chosen to focus on some of the more common types of complements (besides objects, which we already covered in Unit 5).

At this point, it would be useful to distinguish between:

- **complements**, which are needed to make the sentence 'complete' and
- **adjuncts**, which provide additional information but are not indispensable.

Consider the underlined words in the following examples:

1. He wanted <u>a new car</u>.
2. He wanted <u>to drive the car</u>.

Without the underlined parts, these sentences would be incomplete: *'He wanted'. So the underlined words are **complements** of the verb *wanted* — they 'complete' it. Compare these complements with the following examples:

3. He laughed <u>aloud</u>.
4. He laughed <u>at his classmate's mistake</u>.

The underlined parts in (3–4), of course, add more information to the sentence. But, unlike (1–2), they are not absolutely necessary to make the sentence grammatical. You can leave them out and the sentence would still be grammatical: 'He laughed'. So, the underlined parts are not complements, but **adjuncts**, which are optional and can be omitted. The underlined parts in the following are also adjuncts:

5. He wanted a new car <u>for his next birthday</u>.
6. He wanted to drive the car <u>because he loved driving</u>.

In this course, we will not be saying much about adjuncts, because they are less likely to cause errors, and because they are too many and varied. But complements are grammatically much more important, and you should try your best to use them correctly.

Suggested answers

QUESTION 1

There are of course many ways of completing these sentences. Here are just some examples. Notice how the second verb is used.

1. He decided <u>to migrate</u> to New Zealand.
2. He agreed <u>to study</u> harder.
3. He promised <u>to quit</u> smoking.
4. He wanted <u>to become</u> a film star.
5. He intended <u>to beat</u> his opponent.
6. He tried <u>to get</u> her attention.
7. He pretended <u>to be</u> a millionaire.
8. He attempted <u>to extort</u> money from his classmates.

QUESTION 2

There are lots of possibilities. Check with your teacher if you're not sure whether your sentences are correct.

QUESTION 3

All these errors involve the correct infinitive form of the verb to use after the main verb:

1. Blackburn wanted Tom to leave DigiCom.
2. Kevin wanted Angela to marry him.
3. Angela decided not to see her.
4. She told him not to look back.
5. The heat made the mud become rock.

QUESTION 4

The only verbs in Question 1 that can also take an object in addition to the verb complement are *promise* and *want,* as in:

3. He **promised** her to quit smoking.
4. He **wanted** his son to become a film star.

Examples of other verbs that can take both an object and a complement are:
He persuaded his parents to raise his allowance.
She convinced her teacher to give her an 'A'.
The robber forced the victim to give up his wallet.

QUESTION 5

Sentences 2, 3, 5 and 6 contain errors. The correct forms are:

2. I will let him go home early.
3. I saw him pull the trigger.
5. I heard him say that you are his hero.
6. His father will make him go to school.

QUESTION 6

The sentences where the object of the first verb can be understood as being the same as the subject of the sentence, and hence can be left out, are:

7. He likes to be on time.
9. I prefer to have short hair.

As for the reason why the object can be left out in some verbs, let's take *want* as an example:

1. He wanted to become a doctor.
2. He wanted his son to become a doctor.

In (2), the object is 'his son'. But in (1), the understood object is he himself, and since it is the same as the subject 'he', it is omitted. We can think of (1) as being basically 'He wanted (himself) to become a doctor'. Likewise, in 'I want to play tennis every day', the understood object of *want* is I myself.

198 Notes and Answer Key

QUESTION 7

All are correct except (4) and (8). The correct forms are:

4. He wanted <u>to give</u> me a birthday present.
8. She convinced him <u>to marry</u> her.

QUESTION 8

1. I have seen him <u>cry</u> only once.
2. I saw him <u>crying</u> at the funeral. — not much different from (1): 'crying' does not refer to the complete incident as much as 'cry' does.
3. He tried <u>to lock</u> the door. — suggests that he was unsuccessful.
4. He tried <u>locking</u> the door. — does not suggest that he was unsuccessful — probably he succeeded in locking it.
5. He stopped <u>to see</u> her. — He stopped on his way in order to see her.
6. He stopped <u>seeing</u> her. — He used to see her but then stopped doing that (very different from (5).
7. The audience started <u>to applaud</u>. — suggests that this was interrupted or cut short.
8. The audience started <u>applauding</u>. — does not suggest the above — probably they went on applauding.

QUESTION 9

These are just some examples of how to complete these sentences:

1. The Chief Executive declared <u>that some public examinations would be abolished</u>.
2. He assured his parents <u>that he would graduate with first-class honours</u>.
3. He doubted <u>whether anyone would be willing to marry him</u>.
4. He wondered <u>when the recession would end</u>.
5. The officer informed him <u>that his passport had been revoked.</u>

Additional exercises

Here are the original texts. The blanks may be filled by other verbs too, but the form of the verbs should (by and large) remain the same.

Text 1

Before the invention of radio and television, people spent much of their leisure time <u>doing</u> activities that required <u>doing</u> or <u>making</u> something. They practised <u>playing</u> a musical instrument or studied <u>singing</u>.

Most people learned <u>to keep busy</u> by <u>trying</u> <u>to improve</u> their abilities in some way or by <u>practising</u> a skill. People who couldn't afford <u>to spend</u> much money on hobbies often started <u>collecting</u> simple objects, such as matchbook covers or stamps, or even things like buttons or bottle caps. Of course, most people spent a lot of time <u>reading</u>, and <u>writing</u> letters to friends.

Children played games in which they pretended <u>to be</u> pirates or cowboys or people they remembered <u>reading about</u> in books. Many women were extremely clever at <u>making</u> and <u>decorating</u> articles of clothing. Men often kept busy by <u>making</u> toys for children or <u>carving</u> small sculptures out of wood.

Text 2

Eliza Doolittle was a common flower girl who wanted <u>to be</u> somebody. But she had a horrible accent, which prevented her <u>from being</u> accepted by society. So she went to see Professor Higgins, a famous phonetician. She wanted him <u>to teach</u> her to speak proper English, like a lady. He tried <u>to get</u> rid of her at first, but when he saw how great a challenge it would be, he decided <u>to take</u> her on as a pupil. He hoped <u>to turn</u> her from a flower girl into a duchess, to win a bet with his friend Pickering. He promised <u>to give</u> her free lessons. But he gave her a hard time. He forced her <u>to say</u> the alphabet hundreds of times. He made her <u>speak</u> with pebbles in her mouth. He did not let her <u>eat</u> or <u>sleep</u> until she got it right. After a while she decided <u>to quit</u>, but he told her not <u>to give up</u> so easily. In the end she helped him <u>win</u> his bet.

Text 3

The education secretary yesterday denied <u>interfering</u> with the autonomy of two leading universities by <u>voicing</u> support for them to merge.

Secretary for Education and Manpower Arthur Li Kwok-cheung refused to <u>apologize</u> for <u>saying</u> on Friday that he would act as a "matchmaker" to speed the merger of the Chinese University and the University of Science and Technology (HKUST).

"What have I done wrong?" he asked. "What I had done was discuss <u>raising</u> the standards of higher education with their vice-chancellors. It is up to universities now <u>to consult</u> the views of their staff and students on the merger. I will not be interfering with the autonomy of the institutions."

Chinese University vice-chancellor Ambrose King Yeo-chi, who supported the idea, said yesterday the two universities had yet <u>to reach</u> an agreement on the merger, adding no timetable for the move had been suggested.

Professor Li said he had discussed the merger with Professor King and HKUST president Paul Chu Ching-wu after joining the government in August. "We share the same view — that a merger between the two institutions could help <u>develop</u> a world-class university."

He said he had expected his earlier remarks <u>to prompt</u> criticism. "Some people at the institutions may have conflict of interests and self-interests at heart," he said.

Professor King supported amalgamation yesterday in a letter to staff and students at the Chinese University.

"A merger with the HKUST is likely <u>to speed</u> up the process for our university to develop as a world-class university," Professor King said.

But he insisted that the two institutions had not reached any agreement. "It should be decided after <u>consulting</u> staff and students," he said.

Text 4

The United States yesterday accused five Asian nations — China, Vietnam, North Korea, Laos and Myanmar — of severely <u>repressing</u> religious freedom as part of calculated bids to prop up totalitarian regimes.

The State Department named four other states in Asia — Pakistan, Turkmenistan, Sudan and Uzbekistan — as <u>being</u> hostile to minority or non-approved religions.

The report's gallery of worst offenders targeted regimes which it said branded some or all religious groups as "enemies of the state" because of the threat they posed to dominant ideology.

China was accused of <u>scrutinizing</u> spiritual groups and in some cases of "harsh repression".

Vietnam was criticized for <u>restricting</u> religious groups it deems in contravention of state policies. Some ethnic Hmong Protestants had been forced <u>to recant</u> their faith, the report said.

In North Korea the government continued <u>to suppress</u> groups not recognized by the state, the report said.

Myanmar was accused <u>of deploying</u> its "pervasive internal security apparatus" to infiltrate meetings of religious groups and the report cited credible reports that the armed forces had forcibly converted hundreds of Christian tribal Nagas to Buddhism.

The only non-Asian state in the same category was Cuba, where authorities were accused <u>of mounting</u> surveillance operations against worshippers and of harassing unregistered religious groups.

Unit 7: Simple Sentences

In this unit we begin to deal with the **sentence** as a whole. It is very difficult — both in English and Chinese — to define what a 'sentence' is, because it can be extremely complex, as well as extremely simple. So we focus on the **clause** instead, because a sentence can be made up of one or more clauses. A sentence which consists of just one clause is a 'simple sentence', and this unit is about the parts that make up a clause or simple sentence.

We can distinguish five main **clause patterns** in English (following Quirk et al.'s *Comprehensive Grammar of the English Language*). There is one thing that all clauses have in common: they all have a **subject** and a **verb**. In Unit 9, when we talk about non-finite subordinate clauses, you will find that the subject is omitted under certain conditions. But the **verb** is always there. So, remember this, if you have a clause, or a simple sentence, you must have a verb. In Chinese, you may not realize the importance of the verb, because it is possible to have a sentence in Chinese which does not have a verb, but an adjective instead, for example:

他很窮。(He very *poor*.)
我的朋友還在對我生氣。(My friend still *angry* with me.)

But such sentences are ungrammatical in English. You need at least a 'linking verb' like *is/ are*.

Suggested answers

QUESTION 1

The words or phrases which cannot be the subject of the sentence are marked by *, with comments:

1. *<u>Poor</u> are always with us. — an adjective alone cannot be a subject.
2. <u>The poor</u> are always with us. — an adjective phrase with the definite article 'the' can function like a plural noun phrase, and therefore can serve as a subject.
3. *<u>Loudly</u> are here. — an adverb cannot be a subject.
4. *<u>The loudly</u> are here. — an adverb phrase cannot be a subject
5. <u>Some</u> are here. — 'some' is a pronoun here, and pronouns can be subjects
6. *<u>On the table</u> is tiring. — a preposition phrase cannot be a subject
7. <u>Standing on the table</u> is tiring.
8. <u>That oil floats on water</u> is well-known.
9. <u>What he does</u> is well-known. — (7–9) show that subordinate clauses can be subjects.

The generalization is that, besides nouns and noun phrases, adjective phrases with a definite article, and subordinate clauses, can also be subjects.

QUESTION 2

Only the sentences that really need to be completed with an object are given below (the following answers are only some examples):

1. My friend repaired <u>my car</u>.
3. He caught <u>the thief</u>.
7. The building of Disneyland will stimulate <u>the economy</u>.
8. The earthquake destroyed <u>several towns</u>.

QUESTION 3

The sentences which can be rewritten in the pattern Verb-Indirect Object-Direct Object are given below (notice that *no* preposition is used before the indirect object). Those sentences which cannot are marked by *:

1. I sent a letter to my best friend. — *I sent my best friend a letter.*
2. I sent a letter to Japan. — *
3. She baked a cake for her boyfriend. — *She baked her boyfriend a cake.*

4. She baked a cake for the party. — *
5. He bought a car for his parents. — *He bought his parents a car.*
6. He bought a car for transportation. — *
7. He gave a thousand dollars to everyone — *He gave everyone a thousand dollars.*
8. He gave a thousand dollars to charity. — *

Generally, indirect objects refer to humans who receive an object and come to possess it. So in 'I sent my best friend a letter', he/she receives and possesses the letter, but we can't say *'I sent Japan a letter', because Japan is not a person who can receive something.

QUESTION 4

Some examples of subject complements:

1. My neighbour is <u>a witch doctor</u>.
2. In the 1950s, Hong Kong was <u>relatively backward</u>.
3. China will be <u>the world's biggest economy</u>.
4. He became <u>a Christian</u>.
5. These apples are <u>very sour</u>.
6. The students seem <u>nervous</u>.

All of the above underlined phrases are subject complements which tell us something about the subject. None of them are objects, and they cannot be made into passive sentences.

A note on complements

The term 'complement' is widely used in grammar, and may therefore seem a bit confusing to some of you. Remember that the *general* meaning of the term **complement** is: something which is needed to 'complete' something else. Therefore, a complement is compulsory and it would be ungrammatical to leave it out, which is why we're paying so much attention to it. Strictly speaking, objects are 'complements' too, since they are needed to complete a clause with a transitive verb.

QUESTION 5

Linking verbs are marked by [L], and transitive verbs by [T], in the examples below. Both are given if both are possible.

1. He <u>became</u> [L] / <u>saw</u> [T] a doctor.
2. The driver <u>was</u> [L] / <u>injured</u> [T] a man.
3. My classmates <u>are</u> [L] very hard-working.
4. During the trip, he <u>became</u> [L] ill.
5. During the trip, he <u>caught</u> [T] a fever.
6. My teacher <u>wrote</u> [T] a book.
7. My teacher <u>is</u> [L] / <u>married</u> [T] a singer.
8. The truth <u>is</u> [L] that he had an affair with the intern.

A note on the linking verb

The linking verb *be* is a very important verb in English. [We're *not* speaking of the **auxiliary** verb *be* (as in 'He *is* reading'), but the **main verb** *be*, which **links** the subject with the subject complement, as in 'He *is* a teacher'.] Many mistakes are made because students leave it out in sentences like *'Education very important'. A linking verb, like *be* or *seem*, is needed here, even if it doesn't say very much, because English *requires* a verb in every clause or sentence.

QUESTION 6

Only those sentences which need to be completed by object complements are given below ([O] = Object, [OC] = Object Complement):

1. The committee appointed <u>him</u> [O] <u>the new liaison officer</u> [OC].
3. The students voted <u>Professor Lee</u> [O] <u>Best Teacher of the Year</u> [OC].
5. His war experience made <u>him</u> [O] <u>a pessimist</u> [OC].

A note on object complements

Object complements are much less common than subject complements, and are different from them in the sense that they complete what we want to say about the **object** (rather than subject). There are certain verbs, like *make* (in the sense of changing someone or something), which require us to say *what* we 'make' or change the object into — e.g. 'We made John *the leader of our group*'. The object complement 'the leader of our group' says something about the object 'John', not about the subject 'we'. The sentence * 'We made John' would be incomplete.

QUESTION 7

Sentences 2, 4, 5 contain adverbials — i.e. [from the university bookshop], [all the time] and [all of a sudden]. Adverbials are a large group that includes many different things (and *not* just adverbs alone), including the phrases that you saw above. Adverbials have a few characteristics in common:

- they are *optional* rather than compulsory, which means they can be left out if you wish;
- they usually tell us something about the *circumstances* of the event — e.g. the time, place, manner, reason, cause, result, etc.;
- their position in the sentence is relatively flexible, and they can usually be moved around a bit (e.g. '*Suddenly* it started to rain', 'It *suddenly* started to rain', 'It started to rain *suddenly*', etc.).

QUESTION 8

A coordinating conjunction is needed to join the second clause to the first:

6. Vitamin A is also called retinol, <u>and</u> occurs naturally in carrots.
7. The lower part was vegetation, <u>and</u> this vegetation was very thick. [or start a new sentence with 'This ...']
8. Coal is the most important fuel in our daily life, <u>and</u> it has been used for a long time. [or start a new sentence with 'It ...']
9. The baby was very clean, <u>and</u> did not need a bath.
10. The giant plants died many years later<u>. Thus</u> the plants decomposed gradually. [start a new sentence]

A note on coordination

It is very hard to compare sentences in English and Chinese. Part of the reason is punctuation, which works differently in the two languages. In Chinese, it is possible to keep writing sentence after sentence, separated only by commas, with nothing connecting them. In English, sentences are separated by full stops. A **main clause** (that is, a clause capable of standing alone as a complete sentence) cannot occur with another main clause in the **same** sentence, unless they are connected by some sort of **coordinating conjunction** (typically *and, or, but*).

Be careful with *therefore, thus, so*, and such words. They do **not** join main clauses into a sentence. You should **not** write: 'He has no money, **therefore/thus/so** he cannot pay his fees.' You'll need to start a new sentence with *therefore, thus* or *so*. (Alternatively you may use the conjunction *and* before *so*).

Additional exercises

Text 1

I have read with amusement about <u>the</u> attempts of the Hong Kong government <u>to</u> control the littering public by <u>imposing</u> $600 on-the-spot fines.

   As we have all seen by <u>recent</u> reports about beach littering, this system <u>is</u> completely useless as it is.

   I <u>would</u> like to propose a new three-phase scheme <u>which</u> would surely deter littering. Phase one <u>remains</u> the same, an on-the-spot fine, but <u>increased</u> to $1,000. Phase two would be <u>to</u> use the money to purchase a <u>new</u> refuse container to be placed on <u>or</u> near the spot of the crime. <u>On</u> this container would be a small <u>plaque</u> bearing the name of the offender <u>with</u> wording such as "This bin was <u>paid</u> for by (offender's name) as a <u>result</u> of littering." Phase three of this <u>plan</u> would be to make the offender <u>work</u> for one day cleaning the streets <u>in</u> the area where the offence took <u>place</u>.

Surely this would deter littering in <u>view</u> of the punishment and I am <u>sure</u> that it would also severely reduce <u>the</u> likelihood of a repeat offence.

Such <u>a</u> plan would demonstrate just how serious <u>the</u> government is about trying to make Hong Kong <u>into</u> a clean city, if indeed it <u>is</u> serious about a cleaner Hong Kong.

Text 2

The Chinese government will not let just anybody gather <u>together</u> 30,000 people, mostly students, in one place for an <u>hour</u> or two for often emotional motivational speeches. Li Yang <u>is</u> clearly an exceptional case.

Mr Li is the inventor <u>of</u> Crazy English, a language learning method that requires students <u>to</u> shout in order to overcome their inhibitions, and he <u>is</u> more of a proselytiser than a teacher.

He once <u>spoke</u> to 100,000 people in a single day, at three <u>consecutive</u> seminars in Chengdu, and to date as many as <u>20</u> million people are believed to have heard him speak <u>in</u> person or on tape. In perhaps the ultimate official <u>endorsement</u>, he was granted the privilege of holding a seminar <u>in</u> the hallowed grounds of the Forbidden City.

But it <u>should</u> not be surprising that government officials would support Mr Li, China's <u>premier</u> English-learning guru. He is singing their song, and it <u>goes</u> something like this: learn English because it is necessary <u>for</u> your life and your country, and in return you <u>will</u> be rewarded with a higher salary, a stronger China <u>and</u> eventually a future in which people around the world <u>will</u> be required to learn Putonghua just as they need <u>to</u> learn English today.

Text 3

I hope that I am not the <u>only</u> Hong Kong citizen to feel profound shame <u>at</u> the reaction, or rather lack of it, <u>of</u> our community to the bomb disaster <u>in</u> Bali.

The island is a popular tourist <u>destination</u> for Hong Kong people, so it was <u>likely</u> from the outset that some of the <u>victims</u> would be SAR residents. Yet the only <u>response</u> from our city when the news was <u>broadcast</u> was a rather bland announcement on the <u>part</u> of Cathay Pacific that it would send <u>a</u> larger plane than usual to accommodate residents <u>who</u> wanted to return early. While the Australians <u>were</u> sending in medical teams and supplies, we <u>did</u> not even bother to donate as much <u>as</u> a box of bandages.

Are we so <u>wrapped</u> up in the never-ending debates on <u>the</u> economy and negative equity that we have <u>lost</u> all sense of our moral and social <u>obligations</u>? Even when it became apparent that a <u>number</u> of fellow residents were missing, no member <u>of</u> our accountable government was dispatched to the <u>scene</u> to represent our community and to ensure <u>that</u> everything possible was being done to find <u>them</u>.

The Hong Kong community seems to have sunk <u>into</u> a spiritual vacuum. We must examine the <u>reasons</u> for this and try to recover our <u>sense</u> of humanity and compassion for others.

Unit 8: Finite Subordinate Clauses

Sentence structure is a pretty complicated area of English grammar, because a sentence can be extremely long and complex. And mistakes in sentence structure, unlike (for example) tense or number, are harder to correct, because they involve so many factors. The most important things to remember are that:
 (i) a sentence is made up of one or more **clauses**; and
 (ii) the clauses of a sentence are *connected* in some way, either through **coordination** (joined by *and, or, but*), or **subordination** (linked by a **subordinator**).

This unit explores one type of subordinate clause, i.e. **finite** subordinate clauses, which have basically the same structure as main clauses, but with a **subordinator** (like *that, whether, when, because*, etc.) at the beginning. The subordinator marks the clause as a **subordinate** clause, as well as indicates its *relation* to the main clause — e.g. *because* indicates that the subordinate clause is about the reason for what happens in the main clause.

Suggested answers

QUESTION 1

Most of the sentences in this text are neither 'simple sentences' nor 'compound sentences'. In other words, they contain subordinate clauses (which are underlined below). Don't worry if you see a mixture of finite and non-finite subordinate clauses, some of which are not covered in Unit 8. It's enough at this stage to recognize that they are subordinate and not main clauses. The subordinate clauses are underlined below:

The atrocity is above and beyond politics and partisanship. It would not have made any difference <u>if the crime had been committed in reverse</u> — <u>if American terrorists had hijacked Afghan or Iraqi civilian planes and deliberately crashed them into the commercial centre of Kabul or Bagdad with the sole purpose of killing as many innocent civilians as possible</u>. <u>No matter what the cause may be</u>, <u>no matter which side of the conflict is right or wrong</u>, nothing on earth could possibly justify or explain so heinous a crime against humanity. No civilized human being, of whatever persuasion (pro-American, anti-American, Christian, Muslim) would hesitate <u>to condemn it in the strongest possible terms</u>, and <u>to demand that something be done against the perpetrators</u> (<u>whoever they may be</u>). Those <u>who could see something to cheer about at the sight of thousands of innocent people being blown to pieces or burning or leaping to their deaths</u> had better look into their hearts, and ask themselves <u>whether they are really human</u>.

QUESTION 2

The subordinate clauses are underlined below, and marked F (finite) or NF (non-finite):

1. <u>Because he was a tourist</u>, he was easily cheated. F
2. <u>Being a tourist</u>, he was easily cheated. NF
3. He booked his ticket early <u>in order to be sure of a seat</u>. NF
4. He booked his ticket early <u>so that he could be sure of a seat</u>. F
5. <u>Before he went to bed</u>, he usually had a drink. F
6. <u>Before going to bed</u>, he usually had a drink. NF
7. He told me <u>that I should study harder</u>. F
8. He told me <u>to study harder</u>. NF

QUESTION 3

The different parts of the subordinate clause are enclosed in brackets, and marked by a label (S, V, O, C or A) above each part. The 'extra' word (the subordinator) is indicated in bold print.

1. **Before** [the star]^S [arrived]^V, everybody was waiting impatiently.
2. **When** [the star]^S [finally]^A [arrived]^V [in a limousine]^A, everybody rushed forward to see her.
3. The singer had to cancel the concert **because** [he]^S [had lost]^V [his voice]^O.
4. **Since** [you]^S [are]^V [my student]^C, you'll have to obey me.
5. **After** [she]^S [had given]^V [him]^O [all her money]^O, she never heard from him again.
   [NB: 'him' is an indirect object, and 'all her money' a direct object.]
6. The committee told him **that** [they]^S [had elected]^V [him]^O [president]^C.
   [NB: 'him' is an object, and 'president' an object complement.]

QUESTION 4

Missing subordinators are inserted in bold and underlined. If they are optional, they are enclosed in brackets:

1. A large majority thought **(<u>that</u>)** oral skills were important.
2. There are different opinions about **<u>whether</u>** leadership ability is important or not.
3. The majority disagreed **<u>that</u>** an attractive appearance is important.
4. The respondents considered **<u>that</u>** appearance is not an important quality.

5. Scientists find **that** the super carrot can inhibit cancer.
6. Do you know **how** coal was formed? (NB: You cannot have two subordinators, *that* and *how*)

QUESTION 5

Missing subordinators are inserted in bold and underlined. If they are optional, they are included in brackets (which means the sentence is grammatical with or without them):

1. He thinks **(that)** he is the cleverest student in class.
2. She said **(that)** she would come to my party.
3. Magellan proved **that** the earth is round by sailing round the globe.
4. Anne Frank wrote **that** she still believed human nature to be good.
5. He wanted to know **whether** the flight had arrived or not.
6. She wondered **whether** she would win the competition.
7. **That** the earth is round was known to only a few in ancient times.
8. **Whether** he is guilty or not has never been proved beyond doubt.
9. **That** I have not said a word does not mean that I have no opinions.

QUESTION 6

It is important to know that a subordinate clause can function as the subject, object, complement or adverbial of another clause, as if it were a single word or phrase. In sentences 1–4 in this exercise, all the subordinate clauses function as the **subject** (or **S**) of the main clause. You can replace them all with *it* or *this*, or any ordinary subject, like *the rumour, the problem, his action, his last words*, etc.

The following are some suggested ways of joining the two sentences in 5–8 into a single sentence, by turning one of them into a subordinate clause functioning as the **subject** (underlined below):

5. That Hong Kong will be the site of a new Disneyland theme park has caused a lot of excitement.
6. Whether the continent of Atlantis existed in ancient times has been debated for centuries.
7. Why he gave up everything to become a monk puzzles me.
8. What he said just before he died is known only to his wife.

QUESTION 7

The underlined subordinate clauses in (1–5) function as the **object** of the main clause. You can replace them with any ordinary object, like *the answer, the truth, the secret, the trick, his wish*, etc.

The following are some suggested ways of joining the two sentences in 6–9 into a single sentence, by turning one of them into a subordinate clause functioning as the **object** (underlined below):

6. He found out that his wife was having an affair with his boss.
7. Einstein discovered that matter is a form of energy.

8. I cannot read what he wrote.
9. He wants to know whether he passed the exam.

QUESTION 8

The subordinate clauses in sentences 1–5 function as the subject (or object) **complement** in the main clause. They can be replaced by ordinary complements like *a surprise, strange, an old one, puzzling, a madman,* etc.

The following are some suggested ways of joining the two sentences in 6–9 into a single sentence, by turning one of them into a subordinate clause functioning as the **complement** (underlined below):

6. The truth is that no-one can succeed without self-reliance.
7. The real issue is whether we should sacrifice principle to expediency.
8. The reason for his absence is that he had to attend an emergency meeting in Beijing.
9. Our hope is that Mainland China and Taiwan may come to a peaceful settlement.

QUESTION 9

The subordinate clauses in sentences 1–6 function as **adverbials** in the main clause. They can be replaced by ordinary adverbials like *immediately, for a good reason, suddenly, in spite of his poverty, at a young age, selfishly,* etc.

Here are some suggested answers for 7–11, where one of the sentences is changed into a subordinate clause functioning as an **adverbial**:

7. My flight was cancelled because the airport was flooded.
8. He saved every dollar he could because he wanted to put his son through college.
9. The building collapsed before he could get out.
10. Though he lost everything in the earthquake, he is happy to be alive.
11. I saw a terrible accident as I was driving to work.

Additional exercises

Text 1

Three women died and 21 other people — 17 of them fire officers and ambulancemen — were injured yesterday when a fireball tore through a flat where a woman was apparently trying to commit suicide.

The explosion, which rocked the 22-storey building in Tsui Chuk Garden, took place after firemen broke down the door of the flat in a rescue operation.

In the evening, the charred body of another woman was found inside the kitchen of the flat where the blast occurred in block E.

Four firemen were seriously injured with burns to their faces while another seven were in stable condition.

Five other officers were treated and discharged <u>while</u> another was under observation in hospital. Four other residents in the block of flats were injured.

Several of the rescue workers who were injured were in a lift on the way to the scene <u>when</u> the explosion sent it plunging from the fifth floor to the second.

Text 2

China seems to be in the throes <u>of</u> a burgeoning English craze. More than 50,000 <u>people</u> attended this month's Beijing Foreign Languages Festival, <u>where</u> English was the star attraction.

English programmes a<u>re</u> being strengthened at all levels of schooling, <u>and</u> more university courses are being taught in <u>English</u>. With an eye on the Olympics, thousands <u>of</u> police officers, taxi drivers and public servants <u>are</u> being given English lessons.

Of course, it <u>is</u> not for the love of Uncle Sam <u>or</u> English syntax. Learning English is seen as <u>a</u> way for individuals to earn more money, <u>and</u> for the country to accelerate its rise as a world power.

"Li expressly espouses learning <u>English</u> in order to catch up with and <u>overtake</u> the West, a vision he shares with <u>the</u> government and many Chinese intellectuals," said Barry Sautman, <u>an</u> expert on Chinese nationalism at <u>the</u> Hong Kong University of Science and Technology.

Mr Li <u>said</u> that Americans expect Chinese people to learn <u>their</u> language, while they make little effort themselves <u>to</u> learn Putonghua — even while living in China. <u>A</u> Chinese person's first response when meeting a <u>foreigner</u> in China is usually to apologize for <u>whatever</u> English deficiencies they might have. Crazy English <u>specifically</u> targets this sense of insecurity with its <u>emphasis</u> on overcoming shyness.

Text 3

After all, the proposals affect everyone and only fools <u>will</u> say that these proposals do not affect them. It <u>is</u>, of course, true that 99 per cent of <u>the</u> Hong Kong population will never be traitors, or subvert <u>the</u> central government, or steal state secrets.

But do they <u>know</u> that the new proposals will have the effect of <u>eroding</u> the freedom of the press, the freedom of association, <u>of</u> assembly, of procession and of demonstration — all of which <u>are</u> vital to any modern and vibrant society such <u>as</u> Hong Kong? <u>Do</u> they know that if the freedom <u>of</u> the press goes, then no other freedom is safe? Do they know that a community which does not enjoy <u>these</u> freedoms will produce people without creative or independent minds? Do <u>they</u> know that this lack of creativity and independent thinking <u>is</u> causing concern for the governments in Singapore and China?

<u>So</u>, if you want your children and their children to <u>grow</u> up without creativity, please support the proposals.

Unit 9: Non-finite Subordinate Clauses

There are a number of reasons why **subordinate clauses** are even more difficult for our learners than main clauses:

(1) Subordinate clauses can be either **finite** or **non-finite** (the finiteness distinction does not exist in Chinese);
(2) The **form** of a subordinate clause depends on its finiteness, and both types of subordinate clauses are different from each other as well as from the main clause;
(3) The finite subordinate clause requires a **subordinator** (which does not exist in Chinese);
(4) The non-finite subordinate clause requires a non-finite verb, but not a subject or a subordinator (which can appear only under certain conditions).

If you've worked through Units 8 and 9 conscientiously, you should have got a pretty good grasp of their differences. Let's face it: a typical English sentence has a lot more subordinate clauses (both finite and non-finite) than a typical Chinese sentence. That's how the language works. If you stick to a kind of English that has lots and lots of simple and compound sentences, but few complex sentences (i.e. sentences with subordinate clauses), your writing will probably be monotonous and lacking in variety. So it'll be to your advantage to learn how to use subordinate clauses properly. In the following examples, the finite subordinate clauses are marked (F) and the non-finite subordinate clauses (NF).

1. Because he was a tourist, he was easily cheated. (F)
2. **Being** a tourist, he was easily cheated. (NF)
3. He booked his ticket early so that he could be sure of a seat. (F)
4. He booked his ticket early in order **to be** sure of a seat. (NF)
5. Before he went to bed, he usually had a drink. (F)
6. Before **going** to bed, he usually had a drink. (NF)
7. He told me that I should study harder. (F)
8. He told me **to study** harder. (NF)

Suggested answers

QUESTION 1

There are three general differences:

FINITE SUB. CLAUSE	NON-FINITE SUB. CLAUSE
Has a **finite** verb	Has a **non-finite** verb
Has a **subject**	Has **no subject** (normally)
Starts with a **subordinator**	Has **no subordinator** (normally)

QUESTION 2

Julius Caesar was a great Roman general who wanted <u>to **be** crowned emperor of Rome.</u> **Fearing** <u>Caesar's ambition</u>, Brutus discussed with his friends <u>what to **do**</u>. **Drawn** <u>together by their love of democracy</u>, the conspirators killed Caesar in the Capitol.

Caesar's friend, Mark Antony, gave a speech at his funeral. **Speaking** <u>at the top of his voice</u>, he asked the Romans <u>to **lend** him their ears.</u> **Stirred** <u>up by his fiery speech</u>, the crowd then turned on the conspirators. <u>Completely **taken** by surprise</u>, they fled, and a civil war followed. **Knowing** <u>that the end was near</u>, Brutus killed himself.

QUESTION 3

Ungrammatical non-finite clauses are marked with (X):

1. <u>Driving to work this morning</u>, John saw an accident.
2. **(X)** <u>He driving to work this morning</u>, John saw an accident.
3. <u>Disappointed with her performance</u>, the boss decided to sack her.
4. **(X)** <u>He disappointed with her performance</u>, the boss decided to sack her.
5. Peter applied to ten different universities <u>in order to get into one</u>.
6. **(X)** Peter applied to ten different universities <u>in order he to get into one</u>.
7. <u>To be eligible for a scholarship</u>, you have to be a permanent resident.
8. **(X)** <u>You to be eligible for a scholarship</u>, you have to be a permanent resident.

Answer: Non-finite clauses cannot normally have subjects on the surface.

QUESTION 4

The 'logical' subjects of the non-finite subordinate clauses are given in brackets:

1. <u>(John) driving to work this morning</u>, John saw an accident.
3. <u>(the boss) disappointed with her performance</u>, the boss decided to sack her.
5. Peter applied to ten different universities <u>in order (Peter) to get into one</u>.
7. <u>(you) to be eligible for a scholarship</u>, you have to be a permanent resident.

Answer: The 'logical' or 'understood' subject of a non-finite subordinate clause is the same as the subject of the main clause that it depends on.

QUESTION 5

In all these examples, what is wrong is that the 'logical' subject of the non-finite subordinate clause is *not* the same as the subject of the main clause. There's more than one way of correcting the sentences — the ones given (in *italics*) are only suggestions (you may have slightly different answers):

1. <u>Swimming in the sea</u>, the salt water got into his eyes. — *While he was swimming in the sea, the salt water got into his eyes.*
   [NOTE: By having a **finite** subordinate clause, we're able to have a different subject.]
   An alternative: *Swimming in the sea, he found salt water getting into his eyes.*

2. <u>Destroyed by the earthquake</u>, the workers started rebuilding the houses. — *The workers started rebuilding the houses destroyed by the earthquake.*
   [We've turned the non-finite clause into a relative clause which describes the houses directly.]
   An alternative: *Destroyed by the earthquake, the houses are beginning to be rebuilt.*

3. <u>Angered by the noisy demonstrators</u>, the speech was cancelled. — *Angered by the noisy demonstrators, he cancelled the speech.*

4. <u>Talking on the mobile phone</u>, the operation was badly done by the surgeon. — *Talking on the mobile phone, the surgeon did the operation badly.*
   An alternative: *The operation was badly done by the surgeon, who was talking on the mobile phone.*

QUESTION 6

A non-finite subordinate clause can have a surface subject only if the subject is marked by the preposition *for*. (This is a general statement of the most common pattern.)

QUESTION 7

The ungrammatical sentences are marked with (X).

1. **(X)** <u>As having become a citizen</u>, he is entitled to apply for a passport.
2. <u>Having become a citizen</u>, he is entitled to apply for a passport.
3. **(X)** <u>Because having been there before</u>, he doesn't want to join the tour to Beijing.
4. <u>Having been there before</u>, he doesn't want to join the tour to Beijing.
5. **(X)** <u>That being a Chinese</u>, he naturally loves Chinese food.
6. <u>Being a Chinese</u>, he naturally loves Chinese food.

Answer: They are ungrammatical because, in these cases, a subordinator is not appropriate.

QUESTION 8

The non-finite subordinate clauses are marked by (NF). They are all grammatical.

1. <u>Since he became a Christian</u>, he has given up gambling.
2. **(NF)** <u>Since becoming a Christian</u>, he has given up gambling.
3. <u>When you ride a horse</u>, be careful not to frighten it.
4. **(NF)** <u>When riding a horse</u>, be careful not to frighten it.
5. <u>Though he was defeated</u>, he did not lose heart.
6. **(NF)** <u>Though defeated</u>, he did not lose heart.

QUESTION 9

The functions of the underlined subordinate clauses are given in capitals. You can test the answers by replacing them with 'ordinary' subjects, objects, etc. For example in sentence (1) '<u>Space travel</u> is an exciting experience'; (3) 'He hates <u>noise</u>':

1. <u>Flying a plane</u> is an exciting experience. SUBJECT
2. <u>Being chased by a vampire</u> can be very scary. SUBJECT
3. He hates <u>being chased by vampires</u>. OBJECT
4. She enjoys <u>swimming in the sea</u>. OBJECT
5. His favourite pastime is <u>to watch girls passing by</u>. COMPLEMENT
6. His greatest regret is <u>not having studied harder in his youth</u>. COMPLEMENT
7. <u>Attacked on all sides</u>, the soldiers had to surrender finally. ADVERBIAL
8. <u>After finishing his homework</u>, he enjoys watching a movie. ADVERBIAL
9. She opened the door and let the intruder in, <u>thinking that he was her husband</u>. ADVERBIAL
10. <u>Having worked tirelessly for forty years</u>, he finally decided to retire. ADVERBIAL

QUESTION 10

There are several possibilities. Here are just some suggestions:

1. <u>After escaping from jail/ Having escaped from jail</u>, he was arrested again by the police.
2. <u>Upon reading the letter/ Having read the letter</u>, he started to cry.
3. <u>Being a mother</u> is no easy task.
4. She enjoys <u>watching old movies</u>.
5. His biggest achievement was <u>to climb Mount Everest/ climbing Mount Everest</u>.
6. <u>(While) Travelling in Egypt</u>, he saw the pyramids.

Additional exercises

Text 1

Having read the report in yesterday's *South China Morning Post* about abode seeker Wong Lau-shi, I feel both sympathy and disgust — sympathetic towards the mentally disabled deaf and dumb girl and disgusted at the Hong Kong government.

Just what does it take to activate the government's discretionary powers on humanitarian or compassionate grounds? This 26-year-old woman has no one on the mainland **to take care of her,** but has two able-bodied parents who can give her love and support right here in Hong Kong. **If she is sent back to the mainland** with no proper care available, she will almost certainly be taken advantage of in some way.

Text 2

A hidden army of obese Hong Kongers are living indoors for fear of **being laughed at**, says an expert who released figures yesterday **showing** 29 per cent of the adult population is grossly overweight.

About one in 20 adults weighs double their ideal body weight and are classified as morbidly obese, Chinese University of Hong Kong dean of medicine Sydney Chung Sheung-chee said.

"That figure may come as some surprise because **when we walk in the street** we don't see it," Professor Chung said.

"But the truth of the matter is **that morbidly obese patients tend to stay at home**; they don't want to be seen."

Text 3

As the massive Three Gorges Dam project enters its next phase, critics charge that issues ranging from environmental protection to the forced relocation of 1.1 million people have yet **to be properly dealt with**.

"Despite two-thirds of the Three Gorges Dam construction project being finished, problems such as environmental protection and migration are not yet solved," said Kevin Li Yuk-shing, a researcher for the International Rivers Network, a US concern group.

The Three Gorges Dam was begun in 1992 and is expected **to be completed by 2009** at a cost of 198 billion yuan (HK$187 billion).

China hopes the project will control flooding of the Yangtze River and generate 84.7 billion kilowatt-hours of electricity annually, but critics have argued **(that) it could also have a disastrous impact** on displaced people and the environment.

More than 1.1 million people living around the Three Gorges Dam area have been forced to leave their homes **because the land they live on will be flooded** when the dam is completed.

There have been reports of resettlement funds **being embezzled, misappropriated or illegally used**.

Unit 10: Relative Clauses

This unit makes the important point that a **relative clause** and the **noun** that it modifies make up *one* single noun phrase, as in the bracketed portion below:

4. I heard [a song which was composed by a 12th-century nun].

Quite often, students fail to identify [a song which was composed by a 12th-century nun] as a single noun phrase, on a par with [a song] or [a beautiful song]. When you see a clause *directly following* a noun, it is most likely to be a relative clause, so look out for it, and treat all of it (noun + relative clause) as a single unit. This may seem a bit strange for a Chinese speaker, but it's really no harder than getting used to 'He yesterday arrived' (Chinese) vs. 'He arrived yesterday' (English). It's a matter of getting used to this pattern in your mind, and this unit will help you to do that.

QUESTION 1

The subjects and objects are underlined, and identified as 'S' or 'O':

1. <u>He</u> (S) knows <u>the answer</u> (O).

2. <u>He</u> (S) knows <u>that matter is a form of energy</u> (O).
3. <u>He</u> (S) knows <u>the formula which Einstein discovered</u> (O).
4. <u>The rumour</u> (S) is true.
5. <u>What he told me</u> (S) is true.
6. <u>The rumour which he told me</u> (S) is true.

QUESTION 2

The noun phrases are bracketed and underlined below:

1. [<u>The Egyptian plane which disappeared over the Atlantic Ocean</u>] was carrying nearly 200 passengers.
2. [<u>The news which most excited Hong Kongers in recent years</u>] was the Disneyland deal.
3. The teacher scolded [<u>the student who forgot to do his homework</u>].
4. *Life Is Beautiful* is [<u>a movie which can make you both laugh and cry</u>].
5. I can't stand [<u>people who smoke non-stop</u>].
6. He finally got [<u>the job that he wanted</u>].

QUESTION 3

Here are just some suggestions:

1. The bus <u>which goes to the airport</u> is late today.
2. The waiter <u>who spilled soup on the customer</u> was fired.
3. The student <u>who got an 'A' in the final exam</u> was very happy.
4. She married the man <u>who had been her best friend all her life</u>.
5. The World Trade Centre was the building <u>which was destroyed by two planes on 11 September 2001</u>.

QUESTION 4

The 'special word' is highlighted:

1. The Egyptian plane **which** disappeared over the Atlantic Ocean was carrying nearly 200 passengers.
2. The news **which** most excited Hong Kongers in recent years was the Disneyland deal.
3. The teacher scolded the student **who** forgot to do his homework.
4. *Life Is Beautiful* is a movie **which** can make you both laugh and cry.
5. I can't stand people **who** smoke non-stop.
6. He finally got the job **that** he wanted.

QUESTION 5

The noun which the relative pronoun stands for is given in *italics* below:

1. The *movie* **which** won the Best Picture Award was Gladiator.
2. The *movie* **which** I saw last week was Gladiator.

3. The *actor* **who** made me laugh so much was Roberto Benigni.
4. The *actor* **whom** everyone loved so much was Roberto Benigni.
5. The *song* **that** Celine Dion sang in *Titanic* was 'My heart will go on'.
6. The *singer* **that** sang 'My heart will go on' was Celine Dion.

QUESTION 6

The function of the relative pronoun is indicated by the letters 'S' (subject) and 'O' (object) after it.

1. The movie **which (S)** won the Best Picture Award was *Gladiator*.
2. The movie **which (O)** I saw last week was *Gladiator*.
3. The actor **who (S)** made me laugh so much was Roberto Benigni.
4. The actor **whom (O)** everyone loved so much was Roberto Benigni.
5. The song **that (O)** Celine Dion sang in *Titanic* was 'My heart will go on'.
6. The singer **that (S)** sang 'My heart will go on' was Celine Dion.

QUESTION 7

The corrections are indicated in **bold print**.

1. The early symptom of people **who** lack vitamin A is night blindness.
2. One of the plants **which** contains carotene is the carrot.
3. The heat **which** came from the earth would make the mud become rock.

QUESTION 8

1. The movie **which** won the Best Picture Award was *Gladiator*.
2. * The movie won the Best Picture Award was *Gladiator*.
3. The movie **which** I saw last week was *Gladiator*.
4. The movie I saw last week was *Gladiator*.
5. The actor **who** made me laugh so much was Roberto Benigni.
6. * The actor made me laugh so much was Roberto Benigni.
7. The actor **whom** everyone loved so much was Roberto Benigni.
8. The actor everyone loved so much was Roberto Benigni.

Answer: A relative pronoun can be left out *only* if it is the **object** in the relative clause (as in sentences 4 and 8).

QUESTION 9

Answers will vary. Possible answers include:

1. someone who is rich and intelligent
2. someone who is honest and authoritative
3. someone who is knowledgeable and cares about her students
4. a program that entertains as well as informs

5. a place that has ancient historical sites
6. an apartment that has a nice view and clean air
7. books that have an intriguing plot
8. students who are smart and work hard

QUESTION 10

1. Vehicles <u>which are abandoned by their owners</u> will be towed away.
2. Vehicles <u>abandoned by their owners</u> will be towed away.
3. Students <u>who fail the test</u> will be required to re-take it.
4. Students <u>failing the test</u> will be required to re-take it.
5. People <u>who live on Lantau Island</u> are very excited about Disneyland.
6. People <u>living on Lantau Island</u> are very excited about Disneyland.
7. Every suspect <u>who is arrested by the police</u> is entitled to legal aid.
8. Every suspect <u>arrested by the police</u> is entitled to legal aid.

Answer: **Non-finite** relative clauses have a **non-finite verb**, and *no* **relative pronoun**.

QUESTION 11

1. Students <u>planning to study abroad</u> must apply for a student visa.
2. Towns <u>destroyed in/by the earthquake</u> will be rebuilt with international aid.
3. Motorists <u>driving trough the burning tunnel</u> were overcome by the heavy smoke.
4. The most important drug <u>discovered in the 20th century</u> was penicillin.

QUESTION 13

The (b) sentences sound better. That's because the (a) sentences have an **indefinite subject**, which tend to make them sound a little unnatural.

When you try to find Chinese equivalents for the English sentences, you will discover that the (a) sentences, with an indefinite subject, are much more *unacceptable* in Chinese. It is in fact necessary to produce sentences like (b), beginning with '有' (= 'there is').

QUESTION 14

The corrections are given *in italics* below (there's more than one correct answer):

1. * There were over 80% of them agreed with that.
   Over 80% of them agreed with that.
   There were over 80% of them *who* agreed with that.

2. * There were about 23 percent of them disagreed with the importance of leadership ability.
   About 23 percent of them disagreed with the importance of leadership ability.
   There were about 23 percent of them *who* disagreed with the importance of leadership ability.

3. * There are many students study in the library.
   There are many students *studying* in the library.

4. * There was a large number of people worked in the wholesale industry.
   A large number of people worked in the wholesale industry.
   There were a large number of people working in the wholesale industry.

QUESTION 15

1a. A man <u>is washing</u> the car.
1b. There <u>is</u> a man <u>washing</u> the car.
2a. A man <u>has been arrested</u> 20 times by the police.
2b. <u>There is</u> a man <u>who has been arrested</u> 20 times by the police.
3a. A student <u>scored</u> 8 distinctions in the exam.
3b. <u>There was</u> a student <u>who scored</u> 8 distinctions in the exam.

Answer: When we change a main clause into an existential construction ('there is/are ...'), we either (i) change the verb into a non-finite, **present participle** form (e.g. *washing*, NOT *is washing*), or (ii) change the rest of the main clause after the subject into a **finite relative clause** (e.g. 'who has been arrested 20 times by the police', NOT 'has been arrested 20 times by the police').

QUESTION 16

Here are some suggestions (there may be other possibilities):

1. There are 5 books <u>recommended</u> by the teacher as essential.
2. There were many people <u>sleeping</u> on the floor after the party.
3. There was a student <u>who said</u> that the subject was boring.
4. There will be many students <u>applying</u> for the new course.
5. Is there anyone <u>waiting</u> for the bus?

Appendices

Writing Tasks

The fact that this book is aimed at helping you learn and understand more about English grammar does not mean that we are neglecting the importance of **language use.** In fact, as a language learner, it is important for you to realize that acquiring a language comes more from **using** it (in writing, speaking, etc.) than from just learning about it — but with proper guidance as to what is correct and appropriate in the language. This book provides some guidance to help you learn what is grammatically correct in English, but you will need to put this knowledge to use whenever you can.

As an English user and learner, you will no doubt be carrying out a lot of tasks and communicative activities in English both in your study and your everyday life — writing assignments, reports, letters, e-mail, etc. We will not try to duplicate all those tasks in the context of this little book. But just in case you would like to do some more writing, we suggest a number of topics below which might be of interest to you.

Instructions

Write two or three paragraphs, totalling 150–200 words, on any of the following topics. Please note that this is *not* a full essay or a 'research' topic, so there is no need for you to spend time reading up on it. Just draw on your own thoughts and ideas, and try to express yourself as clearly and coherently as you can.

1. Many people have been saying that the standard of English among Hong Kong students has been declining, and that it is not good enough for a world-class city. Do you agree? If so, can you think of any reasons why Hong Kong students' English should be so poor, even after so many years of study in school?

2. What kind of learning activities do you think can best help you to improve your English? Please explain the reasons for your suggestions.

3. Recently, the Hong Kong government decided to introduce an optional (non-compulsory) Common English Exit Test for graduating students in all Hong Kong universities. The IELTS test (originating from Cambridge University and the British Council) was chosen for this purpose. What are your views on the positive or negative effects of such a test?

4. First there was September 11 in New York, and then there was October 12 in Bali. What (if anything) can the world do about terrorism?

5. University authorities today are increasingly concerned about falling standards in student behaviour. Many professors, as well as students, have complained about the chatting, late arrivals, mobile phone use, and other undesirable types of behaviour which go on during lectures, and which distract the attention of everyone, especially those who are serious about studying. Why do you think some students behave like that? What can be done about this problem?

6. One of the more popular ways of learning English is by joining an 'English immersion camp', where students are 'immersed' for a week or two in an environment where English is spoken exclusively, and where they stay together and mix freely with English-speaking tutors and counsellors. Would you like to join such a camp, and what sort of activities would you like to be included there?

Proof-reading Exercises

A 'proof-reading' exercise is one where you are given a text with mistakes, and asked to correct them. It is a useful way of applying your knowledge of English grammar, and testing whether you've got it right yourself.

Read the following texts carefully, and correct all the errors. Then check your answers against the answer key provided at the end of this section.

Text 1

Recently, there is a great debate about whether English exit test should be introduced to test English standard of the university graduates. In fact, the reason for setting English exit test is that the English standard of Hong Kong university student are declining. The government wants to set a test to motivate the undergraduate students to improve English in the university.

However, the government seem to have ignored the drawbacks of the test. In fact, the students do not like exams. What the students would do is to drill the examination skills and forget the goal of learning English. As a result, the English standard of university student will not be raised by the test.

Secondly, they seem to have ignored that the workload of the university students are very heavy. They do not have enough time to drill the English. If the test establishes, this may greatly affect their major studies.

Thirdly, they seem to have equalized the English test result as the English standard. Though the one who score good results in the test could be better in English, this does not mean that the one who get a lower mark is the poorest. Therefore, the test may not be reliable.

To sum up, the exit test should not be established due to the above drawback. Instead, more opportunity to use English naturally should be created on campus to help the students improve English standard.

Text 2

Hong Kong is an international city. We can meet people from different culture easily since many foreigners worked and lived in Hong Kong for a long time. They knew the Chinese culture. We can make friend with them pretty easily. However, I don't think that I would marry someone from a different culture.

Firstly, I think that live with someone from a different culture is difficulty, especially in terms of the eating habit. For example, I cannot eat the Japanese food or pizza everyday because I have some health problem. Also, I am not like eating meat very much. So, I don't want to change eating style.

Secondly, I am weak in language. I cannot listen, read and speak well English. So, I think I cannot make friend with the foreigner. I don't think that many foreigners will be willing to communicate with the people like me because they usually supposed that Hong Kong people can speak fluent English. So, I would not marry with someone from different culture.

Diagnostic Test

We know that all students hate tests (and so do teachers, secretly), but it is useful at certain points in your study of any subject to test yourself, with the purpose of finding out how much you have learned, and whether there are areas of weakness in your previous learning. The following test is designed solely for that purpose. Try to complete it within the time limit given, and mark your own answers by referring to the answer key given at the end of this section. Try to find out where your mistakes are, and look up the relevant sections of the book again to see if you have misunderstood or forgotten something important. If in doubt, check with your teacher.

*Answer **ALL** questions*
*Duration: **45** minutes*

Section One

Instructions: Some of the following sentences contain grammatical errors. Put a cross (X) against each ungrammatical sentence, and correct the error. [NOTE: There is no need to re-copy the whole sentence. You can either: (i) delete the error itself and write the correction (if needed) directly below it, or (ii) insert the missing word (if needed). If a sentence is correct, put a (√) against it.]

1. The booklet distributing to all students will explain everything.
   _____

2. This product is advertise in all newspapers.
   _____

3. My father very angry with me because I came home late.
   _____

4. She tried to buy the book, but was sold out.
   _____

5. This year, there are many people travel abroad.
   _____

6. *Gone with the Wind* is one of most famous movies of all time.
   _____

7. I am strongly agree with you.
   _____

8. Yesterday, I heard him give a speech on TV.
   _____

9. Invention of the computer was one of the great achievements of the 20th century.
   _____

10. Students always like to complain the heavy workload.
    _____

11. After the banquet, the remained food was given to the poor.
    _____

12. His parents persuaded him study accountancy.
    _____

13. At the meeting, the committee discussed about many important matters.
    _____

14. One of my friends live in Taipo.
    _____

15. One of the students won the Young Scientist Award was from HKBU.
    _____

16. The police let the protesters to demonstrate outside the embassy.

17. The building had about 80 storeys high.

18. I heard a big noise last night. Do you know what was happened?

19. The teacher made the students come to class on weekends.

20. The book was very popular, and was quickly sold out.

21. After a long discussion, the plan rejected by the committee.

22. The teacher asked why was he late.

23. The temperature in the desert raises quickly after sunrise.

24. This new procedure can now carry out in many countries.

25. She considers money is not the most important thing in life.

26. They disagree that being educated abroad is important.

27. This book teaches both the speaking and writing.

28. They have too much problems in their marriage.

29. He exercises a lot and eats carefully, and is very health.

30. When did they bought this house?

Section Two

Instructions: In questions 31–50, fill in the blank with the correct form of the word in brackets. [NOTE: Sometimes the correct form of the word may require an **additional** word to be used — such as an auxiliary verb (*is/are/was/were/has/had* etc) or article (*a/the* etc. or preposition (*in/on/at/about* etc.)]

Example 1: The holiday allowed me **to catch** (catch) up on my correspondence.
Example 2: They were **opposed to** (oppose) my plan.

31. One of the students _____ (be) still missing.
32. This shirt is very delicate and should not _____ (wash) by machine.
33. As soon as she started singing, everybody _____ (leave).
34. Students are not _____ (allow) to leave the examination hall early.
35. The shop was full of _____ (smile) salesmen.
36. All applicants _____ (reject) by the selection panel will be notified within a week.
37. His girlfriend wanted him _____ (buy) her a ring.
38. The teacher forced the students _____ (repeat) the exercise.
39. I seem to remember having _____ (do) this exercise before.
40. Your writing is _____ (lack) originality.
41. Most of _____ (foreigner) in Hong Kong cannot speak Cantonese properly.
42. There are thousands of people _____ (look) for jobs in Hong Kong.
43. His parents are very _____ (concern) his marriage.
44. Everybody agrees that experience _____ (useful).
45. _____ (be) the eldest son, he feels the burden of responsibility.

46–50:

In August this year, there (46) _____ (be) massive flooding in central Europe. Hundreds of people (47) _____ (lose) their lives, and hundreds of thousands their homes. Floods of this magnitude (48) _____ (not see) in these parts for a very long time, and the damage amounted to billions of dollars. Not since the Second World War (49) _____ (have) so much damage (50) _____ (do) to these European cities.

Instructions: In questions 51–60, fill in the blank with a word of your own choice *if you think that one is needed*. Otherwise, put a (√).

51. I tried calling him several times, _____ no-one answered.
52. Although he is poor, _____ he is a happy and contented man.
53. Students _____ come to class more than 15 minutes late will be considered 'absent'.
54. I do not know _____ he is guilty or innocent.

55–60:

Earlier this year, the government announced (55) _____ there would be a pay cut for civil servants. There (56) _____ not been a salary cut for many years. I (57) _____ not agree that this should be done through legislation rather than negotiation. Though (58) _____ economy has (59) _____ deteriorating, there are other ways to save (60) _____ money.

Section Three

Instructions: In each of the following sentences 61–74, a number of alternative words or expressions are underlined. Circle the word or expression that best fits the sentence.

61. One-third of student body / the student body / students' bodies / the students' bodies voted for Saturday classes.
62. There were several students scored / to score / who scored / were scored straight A's in their exams.
63. There have / has / are / is many people who believe in ghosts.
64. Meteors fall / fell / falling / are falling from the sky can cause serious damage.
65. George Orwell, that his real name / which real name / his real name / whose real name was Eric Arthur Blair, wrote many politically oriented novels and essays.
66. After the crash, most of the passengers were death / dead / died / die.
67. She is the only survived / surviving / survive / survives member of her family.
68. The scavenger, though living / though lived / after living / lived in abject poverty, was a happy man.
69. After watching the three boys playing in the river for ten minutes, Tom heard one of them shouted / to shout / shouting / shouts that it was time to go.
70. The students elected John / elected John as / elected John to / elected John be chairman of the Student Union.

71–74:

Many people mistake a linguist for someone who is proficient (71) <u>with / about / in / on</u> several languages. They are confusing 'linguist' (72) <u>to / over / with / at</u> 'polyglot'. Linguists specialize (73) <u>with / in / on / at</u> the analysis of language. They may or may not (74) <u>able to / are able to / be able to / be able</u> speak many languages.

Section Four

Instructions: In the following text, words have been omitted at regular intervals. Fill in each blank (75–90) with an appropriate word, which fits the context both in terms of meaning and grammar.

Admittedly, newspapers and authors have to (75) _____ their intellectual rights, but one would like to (76) _____ how these rights are compromised by having (77) _____ article (not the whole paper) photocopied and (78) _____ to a class of students for purposes (79) _____ teaching reading comprehension or generating discussion on (80) _____ issues. Are the students thereby discouraged from (81) _____ newspapers? On the contrary, one should think (82) _____ this would stimulate their interest (83) _____ Hong Kong's newspapers.

Teachers are perfectly willing (84) _____ accept reasonable limitations on the amount that (85) _____ be copied, and on the distribution and (86) _____ of copied materials. But apparently this is (87) _____ good enough. Someone even had the boldness (88) _____ ask, 'Why do teachers have to copy (89) _____ articles anyway? Why don't they write their (90) _____ materials?'

Answer Key

Proof-reading Exercises

Text 1

Recently, there is a great debate about whether **(an)** English exit test should be introduced to test **(the)** English standard of the university graduates. In fact, the reason for setting **(the)** English exit test is that the English standard of Hong Kong university <u>student</u> **(students)** <u>are</u> **(is)** declining. The government wants to set a test to motivate the undergraduate students to improve **(their)** English in the university.

However, the government <u>seem</u> **(seems)** to have ignored the drawbacks of the test. In fact, <u>the</u> **(X)** students do not like exams. What the students would do is to drill the examination skills and forget the goal of learning English. As a result, the English standard of university <u>student</u> **(students)** will not be raised by the test.

Secondly, <u>they</u> **(the government)** <u>seem</u> **(seems)** to have ignored that the workload of the university students <u>are</u> **(is)** very heavy. They do not have enough time to drill <u>the</u> **(their)** English. If the test <u>establishes</u> **(is established)**, <u>this</u> **(it)** may greatly affect their major studies.

Thirdly, <u>they</u> **(the government)** <u>seem</u> **(seems)** to have equalized the English test result as the English standard. Though the one who <u>score</u> **(scores)** <u>good results</u> **(a good result)** in the test could be better in English, this does not mean that the one who <u>get</u> **(gets)** a lower mark is the poorest. Therefore, the test may not be reliable.

To sum up, the exit test should not be established due to the above <u>drawback</u> **(drawbacks)**. Instead, more <u>opportunity</u> **(opportunities)** to use English naturally should be created on campus to help the students improve **(their)** English standard.

Text 2

Hong Kong is an international city. We can meet people from different <u>culture</u> **(cultures)** easily since many foreigners <u>worked</u> **(have worked)** and lived in Hong Kong for a long time. They <u>knew</u> **(know)** the Chinese culture. We can make <u>friend</u> **(friends)** with them pretty easily. However, I don't think that I would marry someone from a different culture. Firstly, I think that <u>live</u> **(to live/living)** with someone from a different culture is difficulty **(difficult)**, especially in terms of the eating habit. For example, I cannot eat <u>the</u> **(X)** Japanese food or pizza everyday because I have some health <u>problem</u> **(problems)**. Also, I <u>am not like</u> **(do not like)** eating meat very much. So, I don't want to change **(my)** eating style.

Secondly, I am weak in <u>language</u> **(English / the English language)**. I <u>cannot</u> **(do not)** listen, read and speak <u>well</u> **(X)** English **(well)**. So, I think I cannot make <u>friend</u> **(friends)** with <u>the</u> **(X)** <u>foreigner</u> **(foreigners)**. I don't think that many foreigners will be willing to communicate with <u>the people</u> **(people)** like me because they usually supposed **(suppose)** that Hong Kong people can speak fluent English. So, I would not marry with someone from **(a)** different culture.

Diagnostic Test

Section One

1. The booklet ~~distributing~~ to all students will explain everything.
   distributed
2. This product is ~~advertise~~ in all newspapers.
   advertised
3. My father ^ very angry with me because I came home late.
   is/was
4. She tried to buy the book, but ^ was sold out.
   it

5. This year, there are many people **travel** abroad.
   travelling / who travel
6. *Gone with the Wind* is one of ^ most famous movies of all time.
   the
7. I **am** strongly agree with you.
8. Yesterday, I heard him give a speech on TV.
   (CORRECT)
9. ^ Invention of the computer was one of the great achievements of the 20th century.
   The
10. Students always like to complain ^ the heavy workload.
    about
11. After the banquet, the **remained** food was given to the poor.
    remaining
12. His parents persuaded him ^ study accountancy.
    to
13. At the meeting, the committee discussed **about** many important matters.
14. One of my friends **live** in Taipo.
    lives
15. One of the students ^ won the Young Scientist Award was from HKBU.
    who
16. The police let the protesters **to** demonstrate outside the embassy.
17. The building **had** about 80 storeys high.
    is/ was
18. I heard a big noise last night. Do you know what **was** happened?
19. The teacher made the students come to class on weekends.
    (CORRECT)
20. The book was very popular, and was quickly sold out.
    (CORRECT)
21. After a long discussion, the plan ^ rejected by the committee.
    is/was
22. The teacher asked why **was he** late.
    he was
23. The temperature in the desert **raises** quickly after sunrise.
    rises/rose
24. This new procedure can now **carry** out in many countries.
    be carried
25. She considers ^ money is not the most important thing in life.
    that
26. They disagree that being educated abroad is important.
    (CORRECT)

27. This book teaches both ~~the~~ speaking and writing.
28. They have too ~~much~~ problems in their marriage.
    many
29. He exercises a lot and eats carefully, and is very ~~health~~.
    healthy
30. When did they ~~bought~~ this house?
    buy

Section Two

31. One of the students **is/was** (be) still missing.
32. This shirt is very delicate and should not **be washed** (wash) by machine.
33. As soon as she started singing, everybody **left** (leave).
34. Students are not **allowed** (allow) to leave the examination hall early.
35. The shop was full of **smiling** (smile) salesmen.
36. All applicants **rejected** (reject) by the selection panel will be notified within a week.
37. His girlfriend wanted him **to buy** (buy) her a ring.
38. The teacher forced the students **to repeat** the exercise.
39. I seem to remember having **done** (do) this exercise before.
40. Your writing is **lacking in** (lack) originality.
41. Most of **the foreigners** (foreigner) in Hong Kong cannot speak Cantonese properly.
42. There are thousands of people **looking** (look) for jobs in Hong Kong.
43. His parents are very **concerned about** (concern) his marriage.
44. Everybody agrees that experience **is useful** (useful).
45. **Being** (be) the eldest son, he feels the burden of responsibility.

46–50:

In August this year, there (46) **was** (be) massive flooding in central Europe. Hundreds of people (47) **lost** (lose) their lives, and hundreds of thousands their homes. Floods of this magnitude (48) **have not been seen** (not see) in these parts for a very long time, and the damage amounted to billions of dollars. Not since the Second World War (49) **has** (have) so much damage (50) **been done** (do) to these European cities.

51. I tried calling him several times, **but** no-one answered.
52. Although he is poor, ✔ he is a happy and contented man.
53. Students **who** come to class more than 15 minutes late will be considered 'absent'.
54. I do not know **whether/if** he is guilty or innocent.

55–60:

Earlier this year, the government announced (55) **that** there would be a pay cut for civil servants. There (56) **had** not been a salary cut for many years. I (57) **do** not agree that this should be done through legislation rather than negotiation. Though (58) **the** economy has (59) **been** deteriorating, there are other ways to save (60) ✔ money.

Section Three:

61. One-third of <u>student body / **the student body** / students' bodies / the students' bodies</u> voted for Saturday classes.
62. There were several students <u>scored / to score / **who scored** / were scored</u> straight A's in their exams.
63. There <u>have / has / **are** / is</u> many people who believe in ghosts.
64. Meteors <u>fall / fell / **falling** / are falling</u> from the sky can cause serious damage.
65. George Orwell, <u>that his real name / which real name / his real name / **whose real name**</u> was Eric Arthur Blair, wrote many politically oriented novels and essays.
66. After the crash, most of the passengers were <u>death / **dead** / died / die</u>.
67. She is the only <u>survived / **surviving** / survive / survives</u> member of her family.
68. The scavenger, <u>**though living** / though lived / after living / lived</u> in abject poverty, was a happy man.
69. After watching the three boys playing in the river for ten minutes, Tom heard one of them <u>shouted / to shout / **shouting** / shouts</u> that it was time to go.
70. The students <u>**elected John** / elected John as / elected John to / elected John be</u> chairman of the Student Union.

71–74:

Many people mistake a linguist for someone who is proficient (71) <u>with / about / **in** / on</u> several languages. They are confusing 'linguist' (72) <u>to / over / **with** / at</u> 'polyglot'. Linguists specialize (73) <u>with / **in** / on / at</u> the analysis of language. They may or may not (74) <u>able to / are able to / **be able to** / be able</u> speak many languages.

Section Four

NOTE: Any word which makes sense in this context and is grammatically correct is acceptable.

Admittedly, newspapers and authors have to (75) **protect** their intellectual rights, but one would like to (76) **ask** how these rights are compromised by having (77) **an** article (not the whole paper) photocopied and (78) **distributed** to a class of students for purposes (79) **of** teaching reading comprehension or generating discussion on (80) **current** issues. Are the students thereby discouraged from (81) **buying** newspapers? On the contrary, one should think (82) **that** this would stimulate their interest (83) **in** Hong Kong's newspapers.

Teachers are perfectly willing (84) **to** accept reasonable limitations on the amount that (85) **can** be copied, and on the distribution and (86) **use** of copied materials. But apparently this is (87) **not** good enough. Someone even had the boldness (88) **to** ask, 'Why do teachers have to copy (89) **any** articles anyway? Why don't they write their (90) **own** materials?'

Bibliography

Modern Grammars of English

For students

Greenbaum, S. and R. Quirk. *A Student's Grammar of the English Language.* Longman, 1990.
Hudson, R. *English Grammar.* Routledge, 1998.
Hurford, J. R. *Grammar: A Student's Guide.* Cambridge University Press, 1994.
Leech, G and J. Svartvik. *A Communicative Grammar of English* (second edition). Longman, 1994.

For teachers

Biber D., S. Johansson, G. Leech, S. Conrad and E. Finegan. *Longman Grammar of Spoken and Written English.* Longman, 1999.
Huddleston, R. and G.K. Pullum. *Cambridge Grammar of the English Language.* Cambridge University Press, 2002.
Quirk R., S. Greenbaum, G. Leech and J. Svartvik. *A Comprehensive Grammar of the English Language.* Longman, 1985.

Books/Articles on the Teaching of Grammar

Batstone, R. *Grammar.* Oxford University Press, 1994.

Bygate, M., Tonkyn, A. and Williams, E. (eds.) *Grammar and the Language Teacher.* Prentice Hall, 1994.

Doughty, C. and J. Williams. *Focus on Form in Classroom Second Language Acquisition.* Cambridge University Press, 1998.

Ellis, R. *SLA Research and Language Teaching.* Oxford University Press, 1997.

Hung, T. T. N. 'How linguistics can contribute to the teaching of grammar'. In J. E. James (ed.), *Grammar in the Language Classroom: Changing Approaches and Practices*, pp. 41–61. Regional Language Centre Singapore, 2003.

Hung, T.T.N. 'Modern perspectives on the teaching of grammar'. In E. L. Low and S. C. Teng (eds.), *The Teaching and Use of Standard English*, pp. 14–24. Singapore Association for Applied Linguistics, 2002.

Hung, T. T. N. 'Interlanguage analysis and remedial grammar teaching'. *Papers in Applied Language Studies*, Vol. 5, pp. 155–68. Hong Kong Baptist University, 2000.

Larsen-Freeman, D. *Teaching Language: From Grammar to Grammaring.* Heinle, 2003.

Odlin, T. *Perspectives on Pedagogical Grammar.* Cambridge University Press, 1994.

Rutherford, W. *Second Language Grammar: Learning and Teaching.* Longman, 1988.

Rutherford, W. and M. Sharwood Smith. *Grammar and Second Language Teaching: A Book of Readings.* Newbury House, 1988.